T0209583

Training Guide for the End Times

Bible Prophecy and America's Judgment

DAVID L. JOHNSON *and*
RICHARD A. HANSEN

WESTBOW
PRESS®
A DIVISION OF THOMAS NELSON
& ZONDERVAN

Copyright © 2022 David L. Johnson and Richard A. Hansen.

All rights reserved. No part of this book may be used or reproduced by any means, graphic, electronic, or mechanical, including photocopying, recording, taping or by any information storage retrieval system without the written permission of the author except in the case of brief quotations embodied in critical articles and reviews.

This book is a work of non-fiction. Unless otherwise noted, the author and the publisher make no explicit guarantees as to the accuracy of the information contained in this book and in some cases, names of people and places have been altered to protect their privacy.

WestBow Press books may be ordered through booksellers or by contacting:

WestBow Press
A Division of Thomas Nelson & Zondervan
1663 Liberty Drive
Bloomington, IN 47403
www.westbowpress.com
844-714-3454

Because of the dynamic nature of the Internet, any web addresses or links contained in this book may have changed since publication and may no longer be valid. The views expressed in this work are solely those of the author and do not necessarily reflect the views of the publisher, and the publisher hereby disclaims any responsibility for them.

Any people depicted in stock imagery provided by Getty Images are models, and such images are being used for illustrative purposes only.
Certain stock imagery © Getty Images.

Scriptures taken from the Holy Bible, New International Version®, NIV®. Copyright © 1973, 1978, 1984, 2011 by Biblica, Inc.™ Used by permission of Zondervan. All rights reserved worldwide. www.zondervan.com "NIV" and "New International Version" are trademarks registered in the United States Patent and Trademark Oce by Biblica, Inc.®

ISBN: 978-1-6642-6333-8 (sc)
ISBN: 978-1-6642-6334-5 (hc)
ISBN: 978-1-6642-6335-2 (e)

Library of Congress Control Number: 2022906844

Print information available on the last page.

WestBow Press rev. date: 05/20/2022

Contents

Acknowledgments

Blessed is the one who reads aloud the words of this prophecy, and blessed are those who hear it and take to heart what is written in it, because the time is near.

— Revelation 1:3

Introduction

It was 330 BC, and the day of reckoning had come for Jaddus, the chief priest. Dressed in his vestments, he led a group of prominent citizens to meet Alexander the Great, whose Macedonian army was approaching Jerusalem. Alexander wasn't the forgiving type, and two years earlier Jaddus had refused to help Alexander's army conquer the city of Tyre, about one hundred miles up the Mediterranean coast.

Submit to Alexander, and he would generally leave you alone, perhaps demanding tribute and some soldiers for his military campaign, but refuse, and there were consequences. The city of Tyre refused and retreated behind its walls on an island. It took seven months for Alexander to construct a causeway to reach the island. When his siege engines didn't do the job, he amassed a fleet from around the Mediterranean to attack the city from the sea. Alexander eventually conquered; he always did.

The consequences to the people of Tyre were grim. Six thousand Tyrians were slaughtered in the fight, another two thousand crucified on the beach, and thirty thousand sold into slavery. Now it was Jaddus's turn, but then something very odd occurred.

According to the noted historian Josephus, when Alexander the Great entered Jerusalem, Jaddus showed Alexander the scroll of Daniel. Josephus wrote what happened next:

> And when the Book of Daniel was showed him [Alexander] wherein Daniel declared that one of the Greeks should destroy the empire of the Persians, he [Alexander] supposed that himself was the person intended. And as he was then glad, he dismissed the multitude for the present.[1]

The book of Daniel was written two hundred years earlier in 530 BC. Convinced the prophecy addressed himself, the twenty-five-year-old Alexander forgave the Jews and proceeded to conquer Persia.

Like Jaddus, we also face a threat today. Only for us it is a potential nuclear war, worldwide pandemic, summer of rioting, and cancel culture. Crazy ideas have become accepted truth, such as gay marriage, transgenderism, critical race theory, and a coming environmental Armageddon. Everything seems inverted and the future ominous. Wouldn't it be nice to have some inside information like Jaddus did from the One who knows and controls the future? You can.

Did you know that the rebirth of the nation of Israel was predicted in the Bible? So is the present hatred of the Arab countries for Israel; the confederation of Russia, Turkey, and Iran; the development of implantable microchips; and the worldwide appeal of globalism. The world is not so threatening when you understand God's plan. As Jan Markell of Olive Tree Ministries says, "The world isn't falling apart; it's falling into place."

What happens if things get worse in the world? We are all accustomed to comfort and order, but what happens if it disappears? Can you persevere? You can if you understand Bible prophecy. You only have one life here on earth; don't let circumstances rob you of your joy. Our training guide can help you live victoriously during troubled times.

Like all successful training programs, our book provides the following key elements:

- **The Need.** Before you train, you must be crystal clear about the need to train. Chapter 1 reveals our need: the disappearance of the Christian worldview from America.
- **The Coach.** You need a coach, a trusted source with inside knowledge to provide a plan for your training. Chapter 2 provides the evidence that such a trusted source is available.
- **The Inside Knowledge.** You must comprehend this inside knowledge to plan accordingly. Chapter 3 explains God's end times prophecies and timeline.

- **The Root Cause.** You won't sit back and do nothing once you realize the cause of this need to train. Chapter 4 reveals how sexual sin has led to God's punishment of America.
- **The Threat.** You can't ease up in your training. The threat is severe. You must recognize that God is punishing America now and will increase the severity in the future. The time and effort to train is justified. Chapter 5 explains how God is judging America and how it all fits into end times prophecy.
- **The Urgency.** You must also recognize that the need to train is urgent, and training must begin now. Chapter 6 reveals the current signs that we are very close to the end.
- **The Opposition.** You must expect headwinds to oppose your training. Chapter 7 reveals the creeping totalitarianism that is spreading across America.
- **The Plan.** You need a training plan to reach your objective. Chapter 8 explains how to prepare for the end times and live a joyful life.
- **The Objective.** To persevere when the going gets tough, you must visualize your objective. Chapter 9 describes our hope: the rapture, millennial kingdom, and new heaven and new earth.
- **The Consequence of Failure.** If you are not yet motivated to train, you will be once you recognize the consequence of failure. Chapter 10 reveals the only way to avoid the coming catastrophe.

This book offers knowledge. With knowledge comes understanding, and with understanding comes peace. Things that go bump in the night are scary until you turn on the light and see them clearly. Therefore, don't fear the daily headlines. Behold God's plan in the pages ahead and face the future with confidence.

1

The Need

T he city is Wroclaw, Poland; the year is 1241.[2] In the town square, cobblestones clatter. A rider on a lathered horse jumps off and cries, "Hear me, brothers. They're coming. The horde is coming. See to your defenses and save yourselves."

The Golden Horde of the Mongols approach. They ride from the east to plunder and destroy, but there is still time to erect defenses. Now is the time to prepare and train. The city must erect barricades, form brigades, learn how to use their weapons, and practice defensive maneuvers. The defenders must stand firm against the invaders.

The Poles faced an existential threat in 1241 when an enemy threatened their way of life. So it is today, only we face a much larger threat, one that affects the entire world.

In a 2013 specially commissioned poll for James F. Fitzgerald, author of *The 9/11 Prophecy: Startling Evidence the Endtimes Have Begun,* Barna Research found that 41 percent of all U.S. adults and 77 percent of Evangelicals believe we are now living in the end times.[3] That was 2013, before the COVID-19 worldwide pandemic, church shutdowns, and punitive vaccine mandates. Surely, those percentages have grown larger today. In this chapter we will disclose that the rise and fall of the Christian worldview in our country is a warning for us to prepare our defenses.

After all, before you train for anything, you must be crystal clear that there is a need. We can find no greater sign that such a need exists than the story of Bruce Jenner, winner of the 1976 Olympic gold medal in the decathlon. His combination of speed and strength made him the epitome of masculinity. Yet, on Friday, April 24, 2015, he made a strange disclosure when interviewed by Diane Sawyer during a special edition of the ABC News program *20/20*. He pronounced, "Yes, for all intents and purposes, I'm a woman."

Rather than disapprove or worry about his psychological state, a couple of months later, *Vanity Fair* emblazoned Bruce, now called Caitlyn, dressed in women's lingerie on its cover. ESPN presented the Arthur Ashe Courage Award to Jenner in July and a standing ovation at the ESPYs. Not to be outdone, *Glamour* magazine named the muscular, six feet two, sixty-five-year-old Jenner "Woman of the

Year." In the 2021 Gavin Newsom recall election in California, Jenner ran for governor *as a Republican.*

Do things seem upside down to you? Boys can become girls, and girls become boys. Men can marry men, and women marry women. Killing a baby in the womb is a woman's right to reproductive health care.

As odd as the world seems to be, maybe events are following what the Bible predicted long ago, as the apostle Paul explained to Timothy.

> But mark this: There will be terrible times in the last days. People will be lovers of themselves, lovers of money, boastful, proud, abusive, disobedient to their parents, ungrateful, unholy, without love, unforgiving, slanderous, without self-control, brutal, not lovers of the good, treacherous, rash, conceited, lovers of pleasure rather than lovers of God— having a form of godliness but denying its power. Have nothing to do with such people. (2 Timothy 3:1–5)

Rather than worry, we propose that you get some inside information about God's plan for the future. What we see today, the Bible has predicted. That is why we must study Bible prophecy.

Maybe you think we are exaggerating, and Jenner is an isolated incident. Let's take a thirty-thousand-foot view of our country's history to better detect a disturbing trend.

Our Once Prominent Christian Worldview

The Judeo-Christian worldview based on the Bible once permeated the United States. Not everyone was a Christian, but even non-Christians held a Christian worldview. It was no coincidence. The first successful American settlements in Virginia and Massachusetts were founded in part to advance the Christian faith, made clear in two documents: the First Charter of Virginia and the Mayflower Compact.

First Charter of Virginia. In 1607, the Virginia Company disembarked 105 colonists at the mouth of the James River in what later became Virginia. What was their purpose? According to the First

Charter of Virginia, King James I granted them land to advance the Christian faith.

> We ... may, by the Providence of Almighty God, hereafter tend **to the Glory of his Divine Majesty, in propagating of Christian Religion** to such People, as yet live in Darkness and miserable Ignorance of the true Knowledge and Worship of God ...[4] (emphasis added)

Mayflower Compact. In 1620, the London Company sent 102 passengers aboard the *Mayflower* to Virginia. They were blown off course and eventually landed on what later became Massachusetts. Their mission was also to advance the Christian faith and was expressed in the Mayflower Compact.

> Having **undertaken for the Glory of God and advancement of the Christian Faith** and Honour of our King and Country, a Voyage to plant the First Colony in the Northern Parts of Virginia ...[5] (emphasis added)

Religious Tests to Hold Office. Although the Constitution prohibited religious tests to hold *national* office, thus to prevent the establishment of a Church of America, the founders felt it was perfectly acceptable to conduct religious tests at the *state* level. Of the original thirteen states, nine had religious tests required to hold office. An example is Article 22 of the 1776 Delaware Constitution that required office holders to take the following oath:

> I, _____, do profess faith in God the Father, and in Jesus Christ His only Son, and in the Holy Ghost, one God, blessed for evermore; and I do acknowledge the holy scriptures of the Old and New Testament to be given by divine inspiration.[6]

Laws Based on the Bible. Most of the lawyers early in our country's history studied English common law by reading the *Commentaries on* *the Laws of England* by Sir William Blackstone, published from 1765 to 1770. The *Commentaries* were infused with Bible verses and biblical wisdom.

In fact, a young, unbelieving attorney named Charles Finney in 1821 noticed so many references to Bible verses in the *Commentaries* that he bought a Bible, accepted Christ as Savior, and later led the Second Great Awakening as its most prominent evangelist.

Student Textbooks Based on the Bible. The most widely used textbooks in American schools from the mid-nineteenth century to the early-twentieth century were *McGuffey Readers*, a series of primers for grades one to six. Approximately 120 million copies of *McGuffey Readers* were sold between 1839 and 1920, placing them only behind the Bible and *Webster's Dictionary* in popularity.

The *Readers* were filled with biblical imagery, stories, passages, and lessons to develop the students' character. For example, a story in the 1836 *The Eclectic First Reader* features a boy named John Jones working for a man who gives John the following advice:

> John, you must always bear in mind, that it was God who made you, and who gave you all that you have, and all that you hope for. He gave you life, and food, and a home.
>
> All who take care of you and help you were sent to you by God. He sent His Son to show you His will, and to die for your sake.
>
> He gave you His word to let you know what He hath done for you, and what He wants you to do.
>
> Be sure that He sees you in the dark, as well as in the day light. He can tell all that you do, and all that you say, and all that is in your mind.
>
> Oh, ever seek this God! Pray to Him when you rise, and when you lie down. Keep His day, hear His word,

and Do His will, and He will love you, and will be your God forever.[7]

Dictionary Based on the Bible. Webster's 1828 dictionary contained voluminous scriptural references, including the following:

> MAR'RIAGE, noun [Latin mas, maris.] The act of uniting a man and woman for life; wedlock; the legal union of a man and woman for life. Marriage is a contract both civil and religious, by which the parties engage to live together in mutual affection and fidelity, till death shall separate them. Marriage was instituted by God himself for the purpose of preventing the promiscuous intercourse of the sexes, for promoting domestic felicity, and for securing the maintenance and education of children.
>
> Marriage is honorable in all and the bed undefiled. Hebrews 13:4.
>
> 1. A feast made on the occasion of a marriage.
> The kingdom of heaven is like a certain king, who made a marriage for his son. Matthew 22:2.
>
> 2. In a scriptural sense, the union between Christ and his church by the covenant of grace. Revelation 19:7.[8]

Colonial Colleges Based on the Bible. Almost all the colonial colleges, including Harvard, William and Mary, Yale, Princeton, Columbia, Brown, Rutgers, and Dartmouth, were founded to train men for Christian ministry. For example, the 1646 Rules and Precepts for Harvard prescribed the following learning objective for students (with the original spelling):

> Let every Student be plainly instructed, and earnestly pressed to consider well, the maine end of his life and studies is, to know God and Jesus Christ which

is eternal life (John 17:3) and therefore to lay Christ in the bottome, as the only foundation of all sound knowledge and learning. And seeing the Lord only giveth wisedome, Let every one seriously set himself by prayer in secret to seeke it of him (Prov. 2:3).[9]

Wave after Wave of Revivals. Great awakenings and revivals rolled across America throughout its history, calling its people to turn from sin and place their faith in Christ.

First Great Awakening. George Whitefield (1714–1770) preached around 18,000 sermons to as many as 10 million people in the Colonies,[10] including many slaves, free blacks, and Indians. The audiences often exceeded the populations of the towns. For example, on October 12, 1740, he spoke before 23,000 people at Boston Commons. Nearly everybody in the colonies heard him at least once.

He even forged a friendship with Benjamin Franklin, who observed the effect of Whitefield's preaching.

> It was wonderful to see the change soon made in the manners of our inhabitants. From being thoughtless or indifferent about religion, it seem'd as if all the world were growing religious; so that one could not walk thro' the town in an evening without hearing psalms sung in different families of every street.[11]

Second Great Awakening. Camp meetings were prominent during the Second Great Awakening, such as the Cane Ridge, Kentucky, meeting in 1801, which attracted 10,000 people. In 1802, one-third of the Yale student body was converted after listening to the preaching of Timothy Dwight, president of the college.

Charles Grandison Finney (1792–1875) was the most prominent evangelist during the Second Great Awakening. At his peak in 1830 to 1831, Finney conducted revival meetings in Rochester, New York. To reveal the impact of those meetings, Finney recounted in his *Memoirs* what a lawyer converted there told him:

"I have been examining the records of the criminal courts, and I find this striking fact, that whereas our city has increased since that revival three-fold, there is not one third as many prosecutions for crime as there had been up to that time. Thus crime has decreased two thirds, and the population has increased two thirds. This is the wonderful influence that that revival had had upon the community."[12]

According to the editors of *Encyclopedia Britannica*, "The Second Great Awakening had a greater effect on society than any other revival in America,"[13] stimulating the creation of numerous organizations to spread the gospel, such as American Bible Society (1816), American Board of Commissioners for Foreign Missions (1810), American Sunday School Union (1817), American Tract Society (1826), American Temperance Society (1826), and the American Baptist Home Missionary Society (1826).

Third Great Awakening. In 1857 the Third Great Awakening began with a prayer meeting organized by a 48-year-old urban missionary, Jeremiah Lanphier (1809–1898), at the Dutch Reformed Church in downtown Manhattan, near Wall Street. Six people attended. A week later twenty came and the next week forty. Soon Lanphier began holding meetings daily, not weekly, and then had to add another room to accommodate the overflow crowds.

Other prayer meetings popped up across New York City, and in six months ten thousand people were meeting daily to pray. The awakening spread across the country and to the United Kingdom. Eventually, an impoverished youth in America with no more than a fifth-grade education, Dwight L. Moody (1837–1899) became one of the most famous evangelists of the era, preaching to crowds of ten to twenty thousand on both sides of the Atlantic. Around 100 million people attended Moody's evangelistic crusades.[14] Moody established what later became the Moody Church, Moody Bible Institute, and Moody Press. In Massachusetts he also established Christian schools for poor men and women.

Twentieth Century Evangelistic Crusades. In the first half of the twentieth century, Billy Sunday (1862–1935) conducted more than 300 revivals with approximately 100 million attending.[15] Sunday claimed that one million were converted, or "Hit the sawdust trail," referring to the sawdust laid down to dampen the noise of shuffling feet in the newly constructed acoustically live temporary wooden tabernacles.

At his peak, Sunday drew approximately 1.5 million people to his ten-week 1916 Boston crusade, the 55,000-capacity tabernacle filled for each meeting. His sermons were printed in the city newspapers where he conducted his campaigns, even crowding out the news of World War I. He preached the saving grace of Christ and condemned drinking. His influence was so great that a Constitutional Amendment prohibiting the production, transportation, and sale of intoxicating liquors was passed in 1920.

During the last half of the twentieth century, Billy Graham (1918–2018) conducted 400 evangelistic crusades in 185 countries and territories to over 215 million people.[16] Three million people committed their lives to Christ.[17] He preached to more people than anyone else in history.

Typical was his May 15 to September 1, 1957, sixteen-week crusade at Madison Square Garden in New York City. Hosted by 1,500 churches, the crusade was televised Saturday nights to an estimated fifty-six million people and drew 2.3 million attendees. On July 20, the venue moved to Yankee Stadium. All seats and the entire outfield were filled. One hundred thousand people were jammed in the stadium, and twenty thousand were left outside, despite a 93 degree brutally hot and humid day.

However, the last one hundred years has revealed a shocking reversal. Once settled to advance the Christian faith, requiring state office holders to be Christians, incorporating biblical truth into laws, schools, colleges, textbooks, and dictionaries, and witnessing wave after wave of awakenings and revivals, our country has abandoned its Christian worldview.

Dismantling the Christian Worldview in America

A quite different climate exists today compared to even sixty years ago. Today, the Christian worldview in America is on life support.

Barna reports that, in the year 2000, 45 percent of Americans were practicing Christians. In 2020 that figure dropped nearly in half to 25 percent. One-third fewer people attended church in 2020 than in 2000.[18] Evangelical Bible believing Christians represent only 6 percent of the US population.[19]

The seeds were sown in the nineteenth century when Charles Darwin's two books about evolution were published: *On the Origin of Species by Means of Natural Selection, or the Preservation of Favoured Races in the Struggle for Life* (1859) and *The Descent of Man, and Selection in Relation to Sex* (1871). These books contradicted the truth of Creation in the Bible.

Higher Criticism. German biblical scholars contradicted the inerrancy and divine inspiration of the Bible in the late nineteenth century. By rejecting the supernatural in the Scriptures and studying sources outside of the Bible, these academics questioned whether the texts were genuine. They concluded that the biblical accounts were mere myths and fables fabricated by ancient sources. They claimed that prophetic books, such as Isaiah and Daniel, were written *after* the predicted events, because in the materialist worldview of German scholars, prophecy was impossible. The beliefs of the German scholars were imported to the United States.

Social Gospel. The liberal mainline denominations transformed the post-millennial views of the Christian church into the social gospel. They emphasized the earthly welfare of people over their eternal destination and need for salvation. They thought that eliminating social evils, such as poverty, child labor, alcoholism, etc., was necessary before people could comprehend the depth of their personal sins, seek a Savior, and thus usher in the second coming of Christ. These beliefs morphed into the progressive politics and liberal theologies that exist today.

Liberal Denominations. Mainline denominational seminaries absorbed the ideas of the German higher criticism and produced liberal pastors who tried to reconcile biblical Christianity with secular science. Surely, man was not utterly lost, they thought, but could be restored by the social gospel.

Wave after Wave of Adverse Court Cases. Since the 1960s, the courts have step-by-step expedited the removal of the Christian worldview from society.

Expunging Prayer from Schools. In *Engel v. Vitale* (1962) and *Abington School District v. Schempp* (1963) the Supreme Court declared that school-sponsored prayer and Bible readings were unconstitutional. Even if the prayer was nondenominational and voluntary, the Court claimed that the state could not condone it, despite the fact that children had prayed in schools for 170 years without any constitutional violation.

Expunging the Ten Commandments. In *Stone v. Graham* (1980) the Supreme Court ruled that a Kentucky statute requiring school officials to post the Ten Commandments on the wall of each public classroom in the state violated the Establishment Clause of the Constitution.

Legalizing Abortion. In the *Roe v. Wade* (1973) the Supreme Court legalized abortion.

Legalizing Homosexual Marriage. In *Obergefell v. Hodges* (2015) the Supreme Court legalized same sex "marriage."

Corrupting Gender. Today, the cumulative effect of these court cases is evident with the public's willingness to accept that male and female are social constructs, permitting a man to become a woman, and a woman a man. In 2021, a transgender woman (biological male) became the assistant secretary of health in the Biden administration, and the House of Representatives outlawed the use of "mother," "father," "sister," or "brother," because they were not gender-neutral terms.

Conclusion

Our country has fallen dramatically in the last sixty years, defiantly violating God's design for men, women, and the family. His punishment is certain as we will explain in chapter 4. However, rather than despair, the believing Christian can take heart that all of this fits a pattern predicted by the Bible. God has revealed history in advance. We watch and wait for His prescribed events to occur. What looks like hopelessness to the world is hope for the believer.

2

The Coach

The citizens of Wroclaw in 1241 must look to a leader for guidance, someone with the knowledge and experience to defend a city against attack. This person must inspire trust, galvanize action, and dispel fear. Such a leader can guide the people's preparation and training to repel the Golden Horde.

So, it is with us. Before we undertake any training program, we need a coach who is a trusted authority and can provide the winning edge. To train for the end times, our coach is God. Are you convinced that God is real, He communicates through the Bible, and the Bible predicts the future? This chapter provides the evidence.

Is God Real?

The evidence that God is real is not hard to find. Consider the following five compelling proofs.

The "Big Bang" Requires a "Banger." We are told by the Jewish Bible, the Old Testament, that God created the universe, and there was a beginning to time. Conversely, the Hindus, Buddhists, and ancient Greeks, told us that the universe always existed. Who is correct?

In 1929 Edwin Hubble confirmed that the universe had a beginning when he discovered that all the galaxies in space were rapidly moving away from us. In fact, the more distant the galaxies, the faster they were moving. It was as though the universe had spewed forth at a single point in time, a beginning. Unable to explain what would cause a universe to burst from nothing by a power outside of time, space, and matter, the scientists called the event the "Big Bang." We call that power God and that event creation.

The Finely Tuned Universe Requires a Tuner. The universe began with incomprehensible precision. If any of the four fundamental forces in physics (gravity, electromagnetic force, weak nuclear force, and the strong nuclear force) were off by an infinitesimal amount, the universe would have collapsed in on itself at the beginning. In addition, very precise laws of physics and mathematics govern the universe. There is order, not chaos. Precision indicates an intelligent source. We call that source God.

DNA Code Requires a Coder. A human body consists of around thirty trillion cells. Each cell contains DNA, a genetic code three billion letters long for creating a human. Only an intelligent source can produce a rational code such as this. We call that source God.

A Complex Machine Requires a Designer. The human body is an incredibly complex machine with multiple integrated subsystems all functioning simultaneously. They must work together or not work at all. The body has a self-lubricating skeleton, a cooling system, a self-repairing chemical processing plant, a visual system that can distinguish among seven million colors[20], a highly advanced sound processing system, a pump that works for up to one hundred years pushing blood through thousands of miles of blood vessels[21], and a central processing system with a storage capacity of 2.5 petabytes (2.5 million gigabytes), nearly as large as the Library of Congress.[22]

A 2,500-square-foot house contains around 3,000 feet of wiring and around 500 feet of pipes. The human body contains thirty-seven *miles* of nervous system wiring[23] and 60,000 *miles* of arteries, veins, and capillaries.[24] Could random incremental mutations over time produce this? Common sense says "No!" Only a supreme intelligence can produce such a complex design. We call that intelligence God.

A Chosen People Requires a Chooser. The Bible states that the Jewish people are God's chosen people (Deuteronomy 7:6–8), and that God made a covenant (oath) with the Jewish people through Abraham (Genesis 12:1–3) and his descendants Isaac (Genesis 26:3–4) and Jacob (Genesis 28:13–15).

Is there evidence today that the Jews are God's chosen people? Yes, very dramatic evidence. Judaism is considered a major religion today. There is 2.1 billion Christians, 1.3 billion Muslims, 900 million Hindus, and 376 million Buddhists in the world today. How many Jews are there? There is only a total of fourteen million Jews in the entire world. Fourteen million! How could such a small number of people receive so much persecution and anti-Semitism?

Individual Jews are among the most successful and accomplished in history. They represent about 0.2 percent of the world's population yet comprise 23 percent of the Nobel Prize winners. The most famous example is Albert Einstein.

Who could cause the vast universe and life to come into existence from nothing? Who could fine-tune and bring order to a universe, establishing scientific and mathematical laws? Who could embed a blueprint and program in the DNA of each cell in the human body to create a living machine, more complicated than any device made by man? Who could choose an obscure group of people, keep them intact for four thousand years, scatter them throughout the world, and reassemble them back from where they started?

The answer is God.

Is the Bible True?

We have produced evidence that God is real, but has He communicated to us through the Bible? If so, we have a trusted source on which we can rely. The writers of the Bible claimed that God spoke to them. Regarding the Ten Commandments, Exodus 10:1 states, "And God spoke all these words." The prophets used phrases such as: "the LORD has spoken" (Isaiah 1:2); "the word of the LORD came to him" (Jeremiah 1:2); "the word of the LORD that came to Micah" Micah (1:1). The Apostle Paul, who was converted supernaturally through a vision (Acts 9:3–6), concluded, "All Scripture is God-breathed" (2 Timothy 3:16).

Evidence abounds that the Bible is true. Here are just a few proofs:

Support by an Immense Number of Copies. Compared to other ancient manuscripts, the Bible was copied more frequently and circulated more widely than any other book in the ancient world. In second place is Homer's *Iliad* with 1,900 manuscript fragments or full copies. In contrast, there are over 23,986 manuscript fragments or full copies of the New Testament and 42,300 manuscript fragments or full copies of the Old Testament, for a total of 66,286 copies to serve as manuscript evidence.[25] (Occasionally, additional manuscripts are discovered, so the totals are therefore in flux.)

With so many copies available, scholars can compare the texts to find copying errors. Through this process, they can produce a nearly 100 percent accurate reconstruction of the original documents, which have long since deteriorated and disappeared. No other ancient book is like the Bible.

Support by Early Dating. Not only are there many more copies of the Bible than other ancient documents, but the New Testament copies are also closer in proximity to their original manuscripts. The earliest copy of the *Iliad* was written on a piece of pottery around 415 BC. The original *Iliad* was written around 800 BC. Therefore, a span of roughly four hundred years separates the earliest existing copy from the original.

The oldest nearly complete copy of the New Testament is the *Codex Vaticanus* dated to AD 325–350. The New Testament was written in AD 50–110. If we pick a midpoint of AD 340 for the *Codex Vaticanus* and AD 80 for the New Testament, the time span between the two is two hundred sixty years. Consider that the copies of the US Constitution we have today are two hundred thirty-four years removed from the original document written in 1787. If the original document was destroyed, and all we had were handwritten copies, don't you think the copies would be accurate despite the passage of time? Yes, of course.

Confirmation by Non-Christian Writers. Since Jesus Christ is the focus of the entire Bible, shouldn't outside sources confirm that someone as important as He existed? The answer is "Yes." Consider the evidence from merely three of the many outside sources:

Tacitus (c. AD 56–c. AD 120), one of the great Roman historians, wrote in his *Annals* about the fire that destroyed Rome in AD 64:

> Nero fastened the guilt … on a class hated for their abominations, called Christians by the populace. Christus, from whom the name had its origin, suffered the extreme penalty during the reign of Tiberius at the hands of … Pontius Pilatus, and a most mischievous superstition, thus checked for the moment, again broke out not only in Judaea, the first source of the evil, but even in Rome …[26]

Pliny the Younger (AD 61–c. AD 113), a Roman lawyer, author, and governor, wrote a letter to Emperor Trajan around AD 112 about a new religious sect:

> They were in the habit of meeting on a certain fixed day before it was light, when they sang in alternate verses a hymn to Christ, as to a god, and bound themselves by a solemn oath, not to any wicked deeds, but never

to commit any fraud, theft or adultery, never to falsify their word, nor deny a trust when they should be called upon to deliver it up; after which it was their custom to separate, and then reassemble to partake of food—but food of an ordinary and innocent kind.[26]

Josephus (AD 37–c. AD 100), a Jewish/Roman historian, wrote the following in his *Jewish Antiquities*:

About this time there lived Jesus, a wise man, if indeed one ought to call him a man. For he … wrought surprising feats … He was the Christ. When Pilate … condemned him to be crucified, those who had … come to love him did not give up their affection for him. On the third day he appeared … restored to life … And the tribe of Christians … has … not disappeared.[26]

Confirmation by Archeology. There are a great many archeological finds that confirm details found in the Bible. In fact, no archeological find has contradicted the Bible. Here are six prominent discoveries.

Old Testament Archeological Discoveries:

- *Dead Sea Scrolls* are fragments, dated from 300 BC to AD 70, from every book of the Old Testament except Esther, and a complete copy of the book of Isaiah, which is nearly identical to the book in our Bible.
- *House of David Inscription* is a stone (Tel Dan Stele) with a "House of David" inscription, dated to the mid-800s BC. King David is prominent in the Old and New Testaments.
- *Hezekiah's Tunnel* is a 1,750-foot S-shaped tunnel, dated to 700 BC, which is mentioned in 2 Kings 20:20 and 2 Chronicles 32:30.

New Testament Archeological Discoveries:

- *The Crucified Man Givat ha-Mivtar* is the skeleton of man, dated to first century AD, with a seven-inch spike driven through his heel, confirming that crucifixion was an execution method, as reported in John 19:16–18.

- *The Pontius Pilate Inscription* is a limestone block with a three-line inscription, reading "Tiberium Pontius Pilate Prefect of Judea," dated AD 26–36. Pilate is an important figure in the crucifixion of Jesus (e.g., Matthew 27:2).
- *The Caiaphas Ossuary* is a bone box with the remains of Caiaphas the high priest dated to the first century AD. Caiaphas was prominent in the crucifixion of Jesus (e.g., Luke 3:2).

The Bible is the most well attested ancient book in existence. Compared to any other ancient document, the Bible has far more copies. Plus, those copies are very close in time to the original manuscripts. Non-Christian writers acknowledge that Jesus is a historical figure, and details of the Bible are confirmed again and again by archeology.

Confirmation by Fulfilled Prophecy. The last proof of the Bible's claim to be God's word is fulfilled prophecy. A book containing predictions of the future that have come true would certainly prove its source was supernatural.

Does the Bible Predict the Future?

In the Bible are eighteen books of prophecy: five major and twelve minor prophetic books in the Old Testament and the book of Revelation in the New Testament. God told the prophet Isaiah:

> I make known the end from the beginning, from ancient times, what is still to come. I say, 'My purpose will stand, and I will do all that I please.' From the east I summon a bird of prey; from a far-off land, a man to fulfill my purpose. What I have said, that I will bring about; what I have planned, that I will do. (Isaiah 46:10–11)

Prophecy is also interspersed throughout the other books of the Bible. In fact, over one-fourth of the Bible is prophetic. Here are just a few prophecies about the Jewish people and Jesus.

Prophecies about the Jewish People

The Jewish People Will Be Dispersed. The dispersion of the Jews was predicted in Deuteronomy 28:62–64, around seven hundred years before it occurred:

> You who were as numerous as the stars in the sky will be left but few in number, because you did not obey the LORD your God. Just as it pleased the LORD to make you prosper and increase in number, so it will please him to ruin and destroy you. You will be uprooted from the land you are entering to possess. Then the LORD will scatter you among all nations, from one end of the earth to the other. There you will worship other gods—gods of wood and stone, which neither you nor your ancestors have known.

The Jews were driven out of their country three times: in 733 BC by the Assyrians, in 597 BC by the Babylonians, and in AD 70 by the Romans.

The Jewish People Will Not Be Assimilated. The Bible predicted in Jeremiah 31:36–37, over two thousand years before it occurred, that the Jews would persevere as an intact people group despite their dispersion throughout the world:

> "Only if these decrees vanish from my sight," declares the LORD, "will Israel ever cease being a nation before me." This is what the LORD says: "Only if the heavens above can be measured and the foundations of the earth below be searched out will I reject all the descendants of Israel because of all they have done," declares the LORD.

The Jewish People Will Return to Their Home. The Bible predicted in Isaiah 11:11–12, over two thousand years before it occurred, that the Jews would return to the land of Israel:

> In that day the LORD will reach out his hand a second time to reclaim the surviving remnant of his people from Assyria, from Lower Egypt, from Upper Egypt, from Cush, from Elam, from Babylonia, from Hamath and from the islands of the Mediterranean. He will raise a banner for the nations and gather the exiles of Israel; he will assemble the scattered people of Judah from the four quarters of the earth.

The Jewish people, along with the Han Chinese, are two of the oldest intact people groups on earth. However, the Han Chinese were not driven from their country only to return again with their culture, language, religious beliefs, and identity intact, like the Jews.

Israel will be born in one day. On May 14, 1948, David Ben-Gurion, the Executive Head of the World Zionist Organization and soon to be first prime minister, announced the formation of the state of Israel. The last time it was a nation was 2,900 years ago. Hours before, a United Nations mandate expired, ending British control of the land. During that same day, the United States issued a statement recognizing Israel as an independent nation. Therefore, during a twenty-four-hour period, foreign control of Israel ceased, Israel declared its independence, and another nation acknowledged the state of Israel's existence. Modern Israel was literally born in a single day as prophesied by Isaiah 66:7–8:

> Before she goes into labor, she gives birth; before the pains come upon her, she delivers a son. Who has ever heard of such things? Who has ever seen things like this? Can a country be born in a day or a nation be brought forth in a moment? Yet no sooner is Zion in labor than she gives birth to her children.

Not only was the establishment of the nation of Israel a miracle, the day after it declared statehood, six Arab/Muslim countries attacked, and Israel miraculously survived, although dramatically outnumbered and outgunned. Israel won two additional miraculous victories against those huge, combined forces in 1967 and 1973.

Prophecies about Jesus

Jesus crucified but bones not broken. King David, one thousand years before the event and even before crucifixion was invented, predicted in Psalm 22:14–16 that Messiah Jesus would die by crucifixion:

> I am poured out like water, and all my bones are out of joint. My heart has turned to wax; it has melted within me. My mouth is dried up like a potsherd, and my tongue sticks to the roof of my mouth; you lay me in the dust of death. Dogs surround me, a pack of villains encircles me; they pierce my hands and my feet.

The fulfillment of this prophecy is recorded in Matthew 27:31:

> After they had mocked him, they took off the robe and put his own clothes on him. Then they led him away to crucify him.

Jesus's bones were not broken (crurifragium) as David prophesied in about 1000 BC:

> He protects all his bones, not one of them will be broken. (Psalm 34:20)

The fulfillment is recorded in John 19:32–36:

> The soldiers therefore came and broke the legs of the first man who had been crucified with Jesus, and then those of the other. But when they came to Jesus and found that he was already dead, they did not break his legs. Instead, one of the soldiers pierced Jesus' side with a spear, bringing a sudden flow of blood and water. The man who saw it has given testimony, and his testimony is true. He knows that he tells the truth, and he testifies so that you also may believe. These things happened so

that the scripture would be fulfilled: "Not one of his bones will be broken,"

Jesus Raised from Dead. David recorded this prophecy in Psalm 16:10 (NKJV):

> For You will not leave my soul in Sheol, nor will You allow Your Holy One to see corruption.

The fulfillment is recorded in Matthew 28:5–7:

> The angel said to the women, "Do not be afraid, for I know that you are looking for Jesus, who was crucified. He is not here; he has risen, just as he said. Come and see the place where he lay. Then go quickly and tell his disciples: 'He has risen from the dead and is going ahead of you into Galilee. There you will see him.' Now I have told you."

For your reference, we provide fifty-two prophecies about Jesus in the appendix to this book.

Conclusion

We have provided strong evidence that God is real; the Bible is true; and the Bible predicts the future. In fact, the Bible contains over nineteen hundred prophecies that either have been fulfilled or will be fulfilled. We have provided just a few of the fulfilled prophecies: the Jewish people's dispersion from Israel, preservation as a people group, and return to their homeland; and the crucifixion and resurrection of the Messiah Jesus. In the next chapter we reveal the key yet-to-be-fulfilled prophecies and where we fit in God's future plans.

3

The Inside Knowledge

The leader of Wroclaw must ascertain what will happen when the Golden Horde arrives. What tactics will they use? Where will they attack? Will they concentrate their army at a certain point and force an entry or will they surround the city and mount a siege? Without this knowledge, the citizens cannot focus their efforts. This, in turn, causes anxiety, conflict, and gridlock.

We too must determine what will happen during the end times. Rather than worry or despair, we can know in advance what will take place and be encouraged. This chapter presents the inside knowledge that our coach, God, has revealed in the Bible. He has provided an end times prophecy and time line. To be forewarned is to be forearmed.

Please refer to Figure 1. Context is important because it indicates where we fit into the overall plan and motivates us to train. We must understand what each element of the time line means, from Christ's first coming, to the rapture, the tribulation, Christ's second coming, His millennial kingdom, and finally the new heaven and new earth.

Christ's First Coming to Earth

The countdown to the end times began with Jesus Christ's first coming to earth. As prophesied in the Old Testament, He was born of a virgin in Bethlehem in around 6 to 4 BC.

Jesus performed miracles to prove He was the promised Messiah and preached to the people about entering the kingdom of God. After about three years of Jesus's ministry, the Jewish leaders accused Jesus of blasphemy, because He claimed to be the Son of God (Luke 22:66–71) and conspired to have Him executed.

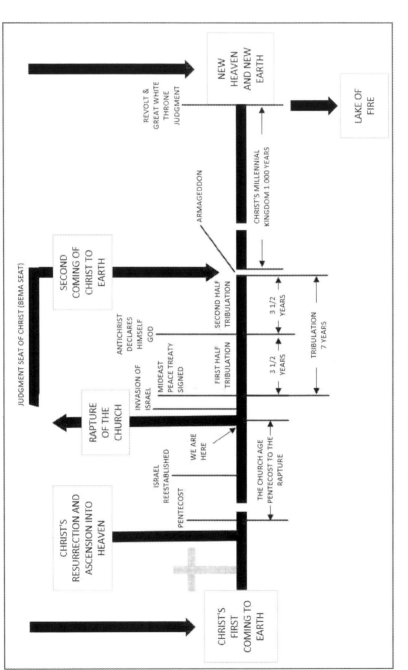

Figure 1 Time Line of End Times Bible Prophecy

Only the Roman government could execute prisoners, so the chief priest and his officials falsely charged that Jesus claimed to be a rival king to Caesar. Jesus was never convicted, but the Prefect Pontius Pilate caved into political pressure and crucified Jesus (John 19:12–16).

This occurred during Passover (Leviticus 23:5), which is important. Jesus represented the final Passover. He was a "lamb without blemish or defect" (1 Peter 1:19) because His life was completely free from sin (Hebrews 4:15). He represented the final Passover lamb (1 Corinthians 5:7), whose blood was shed for our sins.

There were seven feasts, or appointed times, ordained by God on Mount Sinai for the Jewish people, as described in Leviticus 23. The first four of the seven feasts occur during the spring (Passover, Unleavened Bread, First Fruits, and Pentecost). Christ has fulfilled the purpose of those feasts. The final three feasts (Trumpets, the Day of Atonement, and Tabernacles) occur during the fall. Christ will fulfill those in the future.

Christ's Resurrection and Ascension into Heaven

Three days after Jesus was crucified, He rose from the dead, fulfilling the purpose of the Unleavened Bread (Leviticus 23:6) and First Fruits (Leviticus 23:10) feasts. Jesus's body was in the grave during the feast of Unleavened Bread, acknowledging His sinless life (leaven represents sin in the Bible). Jesus was resurrected on Sunday during the feast of First Fruits, acknowledging that all believers who accept Jesus as Savior will likewise rise from the dead in the future.

After Jesus's resurrection, He spent forty days (Acts 1:3) on earth, appearing to His disciples, friends, and five hundred other people (1 Corinthians 15:6). Then He ascended into heaven from the Mount of Olives, near Jerusalem (Acts 1:6–11).

Pentecost

The feast of Weeks, in Greek called Pentecost, celebrated the end of the grain harvest and occurred fifty days after Passover and ten days after Jesus's ascension. This Pentecost foreshadowed the great harvest of souls brought into the kingdom of God during the church age and the gift of the Holy Spirit for all believers.

The disciples met in a house to observe the feast in Jerusalem. Suddenly, a loud noise, like a violent wind, came from heaven. Tongues of fire appeared to rest on each of the disciples as they received the Holy Spirit, and they began to speak in foreign languages (Acts 2:1–4).

The noise attracted a big crowd of Jews in town from many countries, and they were amazed as the disciples spoke in the native tongues of the visitors (Acts 2:5–8). Peter preached to the crowd (Acts 2:14–28). He curiously began with an end times prophecy found in Joel 2:28–32, which predicted signs and wonders (possibly solar and lunar eclipses) that would precede the "day of the LORD." Peter then quoted a prophecy from David in Psalm 16:8–11, which predicted that Jesus would rise from the dead. Peter urged the crowd to repent and be baptized, and three thousand people complied.

With the promised receipt of the Holy Spirit (Acts 1:4–5), the church age began. There are three remaining feasts yet to be fulfilled. Some prophecy scholars believe that the rapture of the church will occur on the feast of Trumpets (Leviticus 23:24). The second coming will occur on the Day of Atonement (Leviticus 23:27), and during the millennial kingdom, the nations will come to Jerusalem on the feast of Tabernacles (Leviticus 23:34) to honor King Jesus on His throne.

Church Age

The church age is called the age of grace because Jesus died on the cross for our sins as the promised Savior. The church age began at Pentecost, as described in Acts 2, and will last until the rapture, as described in 1 Thessalonians 4:13–17.

Israel Reestablished

After the destruction of Jerusalem by the Roman general Titus in AD 70, the Jewish people were dispersed around the world. The Bible predicted in Isaiah 11:11–12 that the Jews would return to the land of Israel.

During World War II, approximately six million Jewish people were killed in the Nazi death camps. At the end of the war, there was an understandable desire by the Jewish survivors to leave Europe and move to Israel. On November 29, 1947, the United Nations General Assembly passed a resolution calling for the establishment of a Jewish State in Palestine, a disparaging name used by the Romans long ago to disassociate the Jews from the land after a Jewish revolt. Palestine is derived from "Philistia," or land of the Philistines, the Hebrew's ancient enemy. The State of Israel declared its independence on May 14, 1948. President Harry Truman recognized Israel within its first hour of existence.

Within eighteen months, the population soared by more than fifty percent. Between 1948 and 1951 700,000 Jews immigrated, and in the 1990s around one million Jews immigrated from Russia alone. Israel grew from 806,000 people in 1948 to 9.3 million in 2020, a mere seventy-two years later.

We Are Here

Many prophecy scholars believe we are very close to the rapture, mere minutes before the clock strikes midnight. In chapter 6 we provide the evidence for this sense of urgency.

Rapture of the Church

The rapture of the church is revealed by Paul in 1 Thessalonians 4:13–17:

> Brothers and sisters, we do not want you to be uninformed about those who sleep in death, so that you do not grieve like the rest of mankind, who have no hope. For we believe that Jesus died and rose again, and so we believe that God will bring with Jesus those who have fallen asleep in him. According to the Lord's word, we tell you that we who are still alive, who are left until the coming of the Lord, will certainly not precede those who have fallen asleep. For the Lord himself will come down from heaven, with a loud command, with the voice of the archangel and with the trumpet call of

God, and the dead in Christ will rise first. After that, we who are still alive and are left will be caught up together with them in the clouds to meet the Lord in the air. And so we will be with the LORD forever.

The word *rapture* is derived from the Latin word *rapturo*, which meant "caught up." *Rapturo* originally was translated from the Greek word *harpazo*, which meant "snatched" or "taken away." The rapture will occur very rapidly, "in the twinkling of an eye" as Paul described in 1 Corinthians 15:51–52:

Listen, I tell you a mystery: We will not all sleep, but we will all be changed—in a flash, in the twinkling of an eye, at the last trumpet. For the trumpet will sound, the dead will be raised imperishable, and we will be changed.

At this time, all believers—those currently alive and those dead—will receive their resurrection bodies ("we will all be changed" referred to above) and lifted up to the clouds, like Jesus when He ascended to heaven forty days after the resurrection:

After he said this, he was taken up before their very eyes, and a cloud hid him from their sight. They were looking intently up into the sky as he was going, when suddenly two men dressed in white stood beside them. "Men of Galilee," they said, "why do you stand here looking into the sky? This same Jesus, who has been taken from you into heaven, will come back in the same way you have seen him go into heaven." (Acts 1:9–11)

Prophecy scholars believe the rapture will occur on the feast of Trumpets because of the "trumpet call of God" mentioned in 1 Thessalonians 4:16.

Judgment Seat of Christ (Bema Seat)

At the time of the rapture, those who have claimed Jesus as Lord and Savior will participate in an awards ceremony called the judgment seat, or bema seat, of Christ. A bema seat in the ancient Olympics was the place where a judge rewarded first, second, and third place finishers. The Greek word *bema* is translated "judgment seat" in English.

> For we must all appear before the judgment seat of Christ, so that each of us may receive what is due us for the things done while in the body, whether good or bad. (2 Corinthians 5:10)

All believers will collectively stand before Christ's judgment seat. The only time it is possible for *all* believers to assemble together is after the rapture. Jesus will judge their motives, desires, and reasons for serving God.

Good deeds, done for God's glory, are exposed. Bad deeds, done for self-glorification, are burned up and not exposed, as disclosed in the following verse:

> If anyone builds on this foundation using gold, silver, costly stones, wood, hay or straw, their work will be shown for what it is, because the Day will bring it to light. It will be revealed with fire, and the fire will test the quality of each person's work. If what has been built survives, the builder will receive a reward. If it is burned up, the builder will suffer loss but yet will be saved—even though only as one escaping through the flames. (1 Corinthians 3:12–15)

Sins are not exposed. There is no condemnation for those who accept Jesus Christ as Savior:

> Therefore, there is now no condemnation for those who are in Christ Jesus, because through Christ Jesus the law

of the Spirit who gives life has set you free from the law of sin and death. (Romans 8:1–2)

The bema seat judgment is for believers. The great white throne judgment, in contrast, is for unbelievers, which we discuss later.

Invasion of Israel

The rapture of the church will profoundly affect the United States' support for Israel. After all, evangelical Christians, the strongest supporters of Israel, will depart with the rapture. This will prompt an all-out attack of Israel by a Russian-Muslim alliance, perhaps motivated by the oil and gas reserves newly discovered in Israel. (Some prophecy scholars place this invasion not before the Tribulation but during the tribulation.)

> The word of the Lord came to me: "Son of man, set your face against Gog, of the land of Magog, the chief prince of Meshek and Tubal; prophesy against him and say: 'This is what the Sovereign Lord says: I am against you, Gog, chief prince of Meshek and Tubal. I will turn you around, put hooks in your jaws and bring you out with your whole army—your horses, your horsemen fully armed, and a great horde with large and small shields, all of them brandishing their swords. Persia, Cush and Put will be with them, all with shields and helmets, also Gomer with all its troops, and Beth Togarmah from the far north with all its troops—the many nations with you. 'Get ready; be prepared, you and all the hordes gathered about you, and take command of them. After many days you will be called to arms. In future years you will invade a land that has recovered from war, whose people were gathered from many nations to the mountains of Israel, which had long been desolate. They had been brought out from the nations, and now all of them live in safety. (Ezekiel 38:1–8)

For the first time in history, these countries have aligned with a common self-interest. Each is listed below:

- Magog is Russia.
- Meshech is Moscow. Classical Greek writers called the people of Meshech the "Moschoi."
- Tubal is named after the Tobol River, on which is situated the city of Tobolsk, once Russia's Asian capital.
- Persia is Iran.
- Cush is Sudan/Ethiopia.
- Put is Libya/Algeria.
- Gomer is central Turkey.
- Beth Togarmah is eastern Turkey.

Russia, Iran, and Turkey have entered into a secret alliance, revealed by a photo of presidents Hassan Rouhani of Iran, Tayyip Erdogan of Turkey, and Vladimir Putin of Russia clasping hands in a meeting in Ankara, Turkey, on April 4, 2018.[27] This has never happened before.

After the rapture, no one, including the United States, will help Israel. She is totally on her own and dreadfully outnumbered. If not for God's intervention, Israel would be totally destroyed. Ezekiel 38 describes how God defeats the Russian/Muslim coalition with a devastating earthquake (verses 19–20), infighting (verse 21), disease (verse 22), and torrential rain, hailstones, fire, and burning sulfur (verse 22). The invasion force is totally destroyed and buried in Israel.

This will pave the way for the Antichrist to rise to power and will allow Israel to rebuild her temple on the temple mount in Jerusalem, now occupied by the Muslim Dome of the Rock shrine and Al-Aqsa Mosque.

Tribulation

After the church (all believers) is taken from the earth and united with Jesus during the rapture, the seven-year tribulation will take place. According to a pretribulation interpretation of Scripture, the church avoids the tribulation, as the following verses suggest:

> They tell how you turned to God from idols to serve the living and true God, and to wait for his Son from heaven, whom he raised from the dead—Jesus, who rescues us from the coming wrath. (1 Thessalonians 1:9b–10)

> For God did not appoint us to suffer wrath but to receive salvation through our Lord Jesus Christ. (1 Thessalonians 5:9)

> Since you have kept my command to endure patiently, I will also keep you from the hour of trial that is going to come on the whole world to test the inhabitants of the earth. (Revelation 3:10)

The phrase "the coming wrath" in (1 Thessalonians 1:10) is literally translated in the Greek as "the wrath, the coming." It indicates a specific wrath, which we believe is the tribulation. Also, John uses the term "church" nineteen times in Revelation, chapters 1–3, and only once more at the very end in chapter 22 but is silent about the church in between, which includes the chapters addressing the tribulation. This indicates that the church is not on earth during the tribulation.

The word *tribulation* appears in the King James Version of the Bible and is translated as "distress" in the New International Version.

> For then there will be great distress, unequaled from the beginning of the world until now—and never to be equaled again. (Matthew 24:21)

This seven-year period is prophesied in the following verse, where it refers to the tribulation period as "one seven," the length of a seven-year "peace" treaty the Antichrist will initiate:

> He will confirm a covenant with many for one "seven." In the middle of the "seven" he will put an end to sacrifice and offering. And at the temple he will set up

an abomination that causes desolation, until the end that is decreed is poured out on him. (Daniel 9:27)

The seven represents seven years. We derive this from Daniel 9:25–26 where Daniel predicts that sixty-nine sevens (69 x 7 = 483 years) will elapse between the decree to rebuild Jerusalem (Decree of Artaxerxes in 444 BC) and the coming of the Messiah (Palm Sunday AD 33). Four hundred and eighty-three years, using the 360-day Jewish calendar, did actually elapse, so each seven represents seven years.* During this seven-year period, there will be terrible wars, famines, plagues, and natural disasters triggered by God's wrath against sin.

Mideast Peace Treaty Signed

The tribulation begins when the Antichrist signs a seven-year covenant with Israel and other countries.

He will confirm a covenant with many for one 'seven.' (Daniel 9:27a)

Who is the Antichrist?

Sometime after the rapture and before the Israel invasion, a ten-nation group, representing the revival of the Roman Empire, will emerge. For background, we turn to chapter 7 of the book of Daniel, written in 655 BC, when the prophet Daniel, a captive living in ancient Babylon, experienced a vision.

Four beasts emerge from a churning sea. The beasts represent kingdoms; the sea represents the world population. The first kingdom is Babylon. The second is Media-Persis, and the third is Greece.

The fourth beast is not described but is dreadful with exceedingly strong iron teeth. This is the Roman Empire. It has ten horns, which represents a revived Roman Empire, perhaps similar to the European Union today. Then, another smaller horn comes up among the other

---

* Using a Gregorian calendar: 444 BC + AD 33 = 477 years; 477 − 1 = 476 years. Only one year elapsed between 1 BC and AD 1. Using a Jewish lunar calendar of 360 days per year: 483 x 360 days = 173,880 days; 173,880/365.25 = 476 years. (There is a leap year every four years.)

ten horns. This is the Antichrist, a leader who will gain control of first three, then all ten, members of the confederation.

> After that, in my vision at night I looked, and there before me was a fourth beast—terrifying and frightening and very powerful. It had large iron teeth; it crushed and devoured its victims and trampled underfoot whatever was left. It was different from all the former beasts, and it had ten horns. While I was thinking about the horns, there before me was another horn, a little one, which came up among them; and three of the first horns were uprooted before it. This horn had eyes like the eyes of a human being and a mouth that spoke boastfully. (Daniel 7:7–8)

> The ten horns are ten kings who will come from this kingdom. After them another king will arise, different from the earlier ones; he will subdue three kings. He will speak against the Most High and oppress his holy people and try to change the set times and the laws. The holy people will be delivered into his hands for a time, times and half a time. (Daniel 7:24–25)

The Apostle John's vision in Revelation 13:1–5 is similar, only the characteristics of the beast are the characteristics of the first three kingdoms of Daniel's vision in reverse.

> The dragon stood on the shore of the sea. And I saw a beast coming out of the sea. It had ten horns and seven heads, with ten crowns on its horns, and on each head a blasphemous name. The beast I saw resembled a leopard, but had feet like those of a bear and a mouth like that of a lion. The dragon gave the beast his power and his throne and great authority. One of the heads of the beast seemed to have had a fatal wound, but the fatal wound had been healed. The whole world

was filled with wonder and followed the beast. People worshiped the dragon because he had given authority to the beast, and they also worshiped the beast and asked, "Who is like the beast? Who can wage war against it?" The beast was given a mouth to utter proud words and blasphemies and to exercise its authority for forty-two months.

The "time, times and half a time" of Daniel 7:25 and "forty-two months" of Revelation 13:15 indicate three and one-half years, the second half of the seven-year tribulation.

First Half Tribulation

One World Religion. Revelation 17 below describes a false one-world religion, outwardly devout, but inwardly idolatrous ("great prostitute"), which will dominate the world ("sits many waters"). Secular leaders will support this religion ("with her the kings of the earth committed adultery").

One of the seven angels who had the seven bowls came and said to me, "Come, I will show you the punishment of the great prostitute, who sits by many waters. With her the kings of the earth committed adultery, and the inhabitants of the earth were intoxicated with the wine of her adulteries." Then the angel carried me away in the Spirit into a wilderness. There I saw a woman sitting on a scarlet beast that was covered with blasphemous names and had seven heads and ten horns. The woman was dressed in purple and scarlet, and was glittering with gold, precious stones and pearls. She held a golden cup in her hand, filled with abominable things and the filth of her adulteries. The name written on her forehead was a mystery: BABYLON THE GREAT THE MOTHER OF PROSTITUTES AND OF THE ABOMINATIONS OF THE EARTH. (Revelation 17:1–5)

A precursor to the one-world religion is the present-day belief system that claims all roads lead to God and all sexual practices and identities are acceptable.

Satan Cast Out. Satan, who had previously stood before God in heaven accusing the believers, is cast out and falls to earth, as disclosed in Revelation 12 below. Satan will ratchet up his persecution of believers ("woman who had given birth to the male child," representing Jesus), realizing the time is short before his judgment.

> Therefore rejoice, you heavens and you who dwell in them! But woe to the earth and the sea, because the devil has gone down to you! He is filled with fury, because he knows that his time is short. When the dragon saw that he had been hurled to the earth, he pursued the woman who had given birth to the male child. (Revelation 12:12–13)

144,000 Witnesses. During the tribulation, 144,000 Jewish men, 12,000 from each tribe, will become evangelists.

> Then I saw another angel coming up from the east, having the seal of the living God. He called out in a loud voice to the four angels who had been given power to harm the land and the sea: "Do not harm the land or the sea or the trees until we put a seal on the foreheads of the servants of our God." Then I heard the number of those who were sealed: 144,000 from all the tribes of Israel. (Revelation 7:2–4)

These men will be sealed, or divinely protected, during the tribulation and will harvest many souls (Revelation 7:9–14).

Two Witnesses. During this period, God will also raise up two witnesses, who will possess great powers, similar to those exercised by Elijah (drought) and Moses (bloody water and plagues). Perhaps Elijah and Moses will actually come back to earth.

And I will appoint my two witnesses, and they will prophesy for 1,260 days, clothed in sackcloth." They are "the two olive trees" and the two lampstands, and "they stand before the Lord of the earth." If anyone tries to harm them, fire comes from their mouths and devours their enemies. This is how anyone who wants to harm them must die. They have power to shut up the heavens so that it will not rain during the time they are prophesying; and they have power to turn the waters into blood and to strike the earth with every kind of plague as often as they want. (Revelation 11:3–6)

Seven seal and seven trumpet judgments will occur during the first half of the tribulation, although some may occur during the second half.

Seal judgments in Revelation 6:1–17 include the Antichrist, global war, famines, plagues, martyred believers, and earthquakes, and in Revelation 8:1 include the final seal judgment, which is the commencement of the trumpet judgments.

Trumpet judgments include hail and fire burning up one-third of earth; a fiery mountain plunging into the sea, killing one-third of the sea creatures; a star falling from heaven, contaminating one-third of the drinking water; severe cosmic disturbances, darkening one-third of the sun, moon, and stars; demons released from a bottomless pit, led by Apollyon, to torment people; angels released at the Euphrates River killing one-third of the world by fire, smoke, and sulfur (Revelation 8:7–13; 9:1–21); and announcement of Jesus's imminent reign, preceded by another earthquake and hailstorm (Revelation 11:15–19).

Some experts speculate that the events of the trumpet and bowl (described later) judgments are descriptions of the sequential effects of nuclear warfare using the language of the first century. Of course, God is quite capable of bringing these judgments supernaturally himself. However, he may withdraw his restraint and allow the sinfulness of man to find full flower.

Some passages that could relate to nuclear warfare include:

- The first trumpet judgment (Revelation 8:7) describes one-third of the trees and grasses burned up, perhaps from a nuclear firestorm.
- The second trumpet judgment (Revelation 8:8) describes one-third of the sea turning into blood, perhaps from nuclear fallout of radioactive dust and ash. (An alternative explanation is that this may be caused by an underwater volcano.)
- The third trumpet judgment (Revelation 8:10) describes "a great star, blazing like a torch" falling from the sky, perhaps from a missile launch. The "star" is given a name, Wormwood, which is interestingly the translation of the word "Chernobyl," a well-known Ukrainian city contaminated by radioactivity from a nuclear reactor accident. (An alternative explanation is that this may be an asteroid.)

Antichrist Declares Himself God

During the middle of the tribulation (three-and-a-half years), the Antichrist will break the covenant with Israel:

> In the middle of the 'seven' he will put an end to sacrifice and offering. And at the temple he will set up an abomination that causes desolation, until the end that is decreed is poured out on him. (Daniel 9:27b)

The following prophecy by the apostle Paul confirms the Antichrist ("man of lawlessness") will desecrate the temple and proclaim himself to be God.

> Don't let anyone deceive you in any way, for that day will not come until the rebellion occurs and the man of lawlessness is revealed, the man doomed to destruction. He will oppose and will exalt himself over everything that is called God or is worshiped, so that he sets himself up in God's temple, proclaiming himself to be God. (2 Thessalonians 2:3–4)

Before the Antichrist can desecrate the temple, Israel must rebuild the temple destroyed in AD 70. Plans are now underway to furnish a rebuilt temple and resume sacrifices. For example, on Hanukah, December 10, 2018, an activist group in Israel built and dedicated an altar for the new temple.[28] In addition, the Temple Institute has imported frozen embryos and implanted them in Israeli cows, and an entirely red calf was born (one with no more than two non-red hairs on its body) as required by Numbers 19:1–3.[29]

A false prophet will also emerge, someone who is appealing, a great preacher, orator, and cunning deceiver. He will force the world to worship the Antichrist. Empowered by Satan, the false prophet will produce miraculous signs and set up an idol (image of the beast) that can talk and condemn to death those who refuse to worship the Antichrist. Perhaps this image is an android, human-animal hybrid, or a hologram powered by artificial intelligence.

> Then I saw a second beast, coming out of the earth. It had two horns like a lamb, but it spoke like a dragon. It exercised all the authority of the first beast on its behalf, and made the earth and its inhabitants worship the first beast, whose fatal wound had been healed. And it performed great signs, even causing fire to come down from heaven to the earth in full view of the people. Because of the signs it was given power to perform on behalf of the first beast, it deceived the inhabitants of the earth. It ordered them to set up an image in honor of the beast who was wounded by the sword and yet lived. The second beast was given power to give breath to the image of the first beast, so that the image could speak and cause all who refused to worship the image to be killed. (Revelation 13:11–15)

Towards the end of Revelation 17, the Antichrist and his revived Roman Empire leaders ("beast and the ten horns") will turn on and destroy the false one-world religion. The beast (Antichrist) will no longer tolerate a counterfeit religion. He will declare himself to be God and demand worship.

> The beast and the ten horns you saw will hate the prostitute. They will bring her to ruin and leave her naked; they will eat her flesh and burn her with fire. For God has put it into their hearts to accomplish his purpose by agreeing to hand over to the beast their royal authority, until God's words are fulfilled. (Revelation 17:16–17)

The Antichrist will kill the two witnesses. The bodies will lie in Jerusalem for the world to view for three-and-one-half days. Then, God will resurrect them to heaven as an amazed world watches.

> Now when they have finished their testimony, the beast that comes up from the Abyss will attack them, and overpower and kill them. Their bodies will lie in the public square of the great city—which is figuratively called Sodom and Egypt—where also their Lord was crucified. For three and a half days some from every people, tribe, language and nation will gaze on their bodies and refuse them burial. The inhabitants of the earth will gloat over them and will celebrate by sending each other gifts, because these two prophets had tormented those who live on the earth. But after the three and a half days the breath of life from God entered them, and they stood on their feet, and terror struck those who saw them. Then they heard a loud voice from heaven saying to them, "Come up here." And they went up to heaven in a cloud, while their enemies looked on. (Revelation 11:7–12)

Second Half Tribulation

Mark of the Beast. All people must worship the Antichrist and as evidence, must receive the mark of the beast, a visible mark, like a tattoo.

In addition, those people will receive a "commerce passport," perhaps resembling a RFID chip implant.

> It also forced all people, great and small, rich and poor, free and slave, to receive a mark on their right hands or on their foreheads, so that they could not buy or sell unless they had the mark, which is the name of the beast or the number of its name. This calls for wisdom. Let the person who has insight calculate the number of the beast, for it is the number of a man. That number is 666. (Revelation 13:16–18)

The technology is here. The Swedes have used it since 2015. They insert a tiny microchip, the size of a grain of rice, under the skin, precluding the need to carry keys, credit cards, and train tickets. In 2018 the Swedes injected microchips into the hands of three thousand citizens, who then use the implanted chips to board trains after making reservations online. Conductors merely scan the passenger's hand when boarding.[30]

A series of bowl judgments occur. Painful sores plague the population; the sea is contaminated, killing the sea life; rivers and springs are contaminated, destroying drinking water; the sun scorches people; the world is plunged into darkness; the Euphrates river dries up, and demonic spirits gather the kings of the world at Armageddon; a great earthquake occurs unlike any in history that levels cities, mountains, and islands; and one-hundred-pound hailstones fall on the people (Revelation 16:2–21).

The bowl judgments could result from the lingering effects of radioactivity, more intense and deadly than the nuclear explosions purportedly described by the trumpet judgments.

- The first bowl judgment (Revelation 16:2) describes "festering sores," perhaps from radiation burns.
- The fourth bowl judgment (Revelation 16:8) states "the sun was allowed to scorch people with fire," perhaps from a depletion of the earth's ozone layer by radiation.

Zechariah 14:12 describes an end-time plague that also may relate to nuclear radiation and affects both humans and animals.

> This is the plague with which the Lord will strike all the nations that fought against Jerusalem: Their flesh will rot while they are still standing on their feet, their eyes will rot in their sockets, and their tongues will rot in their mouths.

Armageddon

Armageddon means "Mount of Megiddo" and is located about sixty miles north of Jerusalem. The nations of the world, perhaps with the United States, gather at Armageddon to destroy the Jews.

> Then they gathered the kings together to the place that in Hebrew is called Armageddon. (Revelation 16:16)

A dried-up Euphrates River facilitates the transport of mighty armies. Only the second coming of Jesus will prevent the obliteration of the Jewish people.

Those heeding Jesus's warning to flee to the mountains (Matthew 24:15–20) after the temple is desecrated will find a place of refuge prepared by God:

> The woman fled into the wilderness to a place prepared for her by God, where she might be taken care of for 1,260 days. (Revelation 12:6)

This woman represents Israel, not to be confused with the woman sitting on the scarlet beast, which represents the false religion. Trapped by overwhelming force, the Jewish remnant will cry out to God for salvation (Hosea 6:1–3).

Second Coming of Jesus

Jesus comes to earth a second time as a conquering king, when he arrives with the armies of heaven.

46

Then will appear the sign of the Son of Man in heaven. And then all the peoples of the earth will mourn when they see the Son of Man coming on the clouds of heaven, with power and great glory. (Matthew 24:30)

"Look, he is coming with the clouds," and "every eye will see him, even those who pierced him"; and all peoples on earth "will mourn because of him." So shall it be! Amen. (Revelation 1:7)

A more detailed description of Jesus's second coming is found in the following verses. The raptured saints ("armies of heaven...dressed in fine linen, white and clean") will return with Jesus, joined by the saints who died during the tribulation, to rule during the millennial kingdom:

I saw heaven standing open and there before me was a white horse, whose rider is called Faithful and True. With justice he judges and wages war. His eyes are like blazing fire, and on his head are many crowns. He has a name written on him that no one knows but he himself. He is dressed in a robe dipped in blood, and his name is the Word of God. The armies of heaven were following him, riding on white horses and dressed in fine linen, white and clean. Coming out of his mouth is a sharp sword with which to strike down the nations. "He will rule them with an iron scepter." He treads the winepress of the fury of the wrath of God Almighty. On his robe and on his thigh he has this name written: KING OF KINGS AND LORD OF LORDS. (Revelation 19:11–16)

John refers to Jesus as the Word of God in John 1:1, 14.

Jesus will defeat the Antichrist and his army, cast the Antichrist and the false prophet into the lake of fire, and end the tribulation:

Then I saw the beast and the kings of the earth and their armies gathered together to wage war against the rider

47

on the horse and his army. But the beast was captured, and with it the false prophet who had performed the signs on its behalf. With these signs he had deluded those who had received the mark of the beast and worshiped its image. The two of them were thrown alive into the fiery lake of burning sulfur. The rest were killed with the sword coming out of the mouth of the rider on the horse, and all the birds gorged themselves on their flesh. (Revelation 19:19–21)

Satan Bound. Satan will be bound for a thousand years:

And I saw an angel coming down out of heaven, having the key to the Abyss and holding in his hand a great chain. He seized the dragon, that ancient serpent, who is the devil, or Satan, and bound him for a thousand years. He threw him into the Abyss, and locked and sealed it over him, to keep him from deceiving the nations anymore until the thousand years were ended. After that, he must be set free for a short time. (Revelation 20:1–3)

Sheep and Goats Judgment. Jesus will judge the nations, as specified in Matthew 25:31–46. Christ will place the sheep on His right and the goats on His left. The sheep represent believers who came to the aid of persecuted Jewish brothers during the tribulation. The unbelieving goats refused to aid the Jewish brothers. The sheep are welcomed into the millennial kingdom. The goats are sent to eternal punishment.

The marriage supper of the lamb will likely occur during this period:

Let us rejoice and be glad and give him glory! For the wedding of the Lamb has come, and his bride has made herself ready. Fine linen, bright and clean, was given her to wear." (Fine linen stands for the righteous acts of God's holy people.) Then the angel said to me, "Write this: Blessed are those who are invited to the wedding supper of the Lamb!" And he added, "These are the true words of God." (Revelation 19:7–9)

Millennial Kingdom

Jesus will begin His millennial reign, lasting one thousand years.

> I saw thrones on which were seated those who had been given authority to judge. And I saw the souls of those who had been beheaded because of their testimony about Jesus and because of the word of God. They had not worshiped the beast or its image and had not received its mark on their foreheads or their hands. They came to life and reigned with Christ a thousand years. (Revelation 20:4)

Mortal believers, both Gentile and Jew, who have survived the tribulation, will enter the millennial kingdom to live, have children, and die, although with longer life spans.

Jesus will reign on David's throne in Jerusalem.

> For to us a child is born, to us a son is given, and the government will be on his shoulders. And he will be called Wonderful Counselor, Mighty God, Everlasting Father, Prince of Peace. Of the greatness of his government and peace there will be no end. He will reign on David's throne and over his kingdom, establishing and upholding it with justice and righteousness from that time on and forever. The zeal of the Lord Almighty will accomplish this. (Isaiah 9:6–7)

The thousand years will be a time of peace, when even animals will stop killing and eating each other.

> The wolf will live with the lamb, the leopard will lie down with the goat, the calf and the lion and the

yearling together; and a little child will lead them. The cow will feed with the bear, their young will lie down together, and the lion will eat straw like the ox. (Isaiah 11:6–7)

Great White Throne Judgment

At the end of the millennial reign of Jesus, God releases Satan, who was bound during the one thousand years. Satan will deceive people again, cause one more rebellion against the Lord, but will be quickly defeated:

> When the thousand years are over, Satan will be released from his prison and will go out to deceive the nations in the four corners of the earth—Gog and Magog—and to gather them for battle. In number they are like the sand on the seashore. They marched across the breadth of the earth and surrounded the camp of God's people, the city he loves. But fire came down from heaven and devoured them. And the devil, who deceived them, was thrown into the lake of burning sulfur, where the beast and the false prophet had been thrown. They will be tormented day and night for ever and ever. (Revelation 20:7–10)

During the millennial kingdom, some people will sin and reject Jesus, despite the perfect conditions in the world. This proves conclusively that humans need a Savior. All humans are inherently sinful and incapable of perfecting themselves, even in a perfect society.

The final judgment of all *unbelievers* is called the great white throne judgment. It is described in Revelation 20:11–13:

> Then I saw a great white throne and him who was seated on it. The earth and the heavens fled from his presence, and there was no place for them. And I saw the dead, great and small, standing before the throne, and books were opened. Another book was opened, which is the book of life. The dead were judged according to what

they had done as recorded in the books. The sea gave up the dead that were in it, and death and Hades gave up the dead that were in them, and each person was judged according to what they had done.

All people will appear in a courtroom-like setting before God, the divine judge. Each sinner comes before the bar of God. Books are opened, and nonbelievers are judged according to their works, but of course works will not save them.

Another book, called the Book of Life is also opened. The Book of Life is mentioned throughout the Bible. For example, the prophet Daniel wrote:

> At that time Michael, the great prince who protects your people, will arise. There will be a time of distress such as has not happened from the beginning of nations until then. But at that time your people—everyone whose name is found written in the book—will be delivered. (Daniel 12:1)

People whose names are written in the Book of Life are spared and excluded from the great white throne judgment.

Lake of Fire

All people whose names are not written in the Book of Life will be condemned and thrown into the lake of fire:

> Then death and Hades were thrown into the lake of fire. The lake of fire is the second death. Anyone whose name was not found written in the book of life was thrown into the lake of fire. (Revelation 20:14–15)

New Heaven and New Earth

Once all unsaved sinners, Satan, and his demons are cast into the lake of fire, God will finalize the roster of those who will live with Him for eternity. At this time, He will demolish the old universe and restore it to the pristine condition of Eden. This was prophesied by Isaiah in the 700s BC:

> See, I will create new heavens and a new earth. The former things will not be remembered, nor will they come to mind. (Isaiah 65:17)

This was also prophesied by the apostle Peter in the AD 60s:

> But the day of the Lord will come like a thief. The heavens will disappear with a roar; the elements will be destroyed by fire, and the earth and everything done in it will be laid bare. Since everything will be destroyed in this way, what kind of people ought you to be? You ought to live holy and godly lives as you look forward to the day of God and speed its coming. That day will bring about the destruction of the heavens by fire, and the elements will melt in the heat. But in keeping with his promise we are looking forward to a new heaven and a new earth, where righteousness dwells. (2 Peter 3:10–13)

The apostle John describes his vision about the new heaven and new earth:

> Then I saw "a new heaven and a new earth," for the first heaven and the first earth had passed away, and there was no longer any sea. I saw the Holy City, the new Jerusalem, coming down out of heaven from God, prepared as a bride beautifully dressed for her husband. And I heard a loud voice from the throne saying, "Look! God's dwelling place is now among the people, and he will dwell with them. They will be his people, and God himself will be with them and be their God. 'He will wipe every tear from their eyes. There will be no more death' or mourning or crying or pain, for the old order of things has passed away." (Revelation 21:1–4)

This is ultimately our final goal, the new heaven and new earth, where we will live with Jesus forever.

Conclusion

We have revealed the inside information about the future that God has revealed in the Bible. By piecing together passages in the Old and New Testaments, we can sequence the events that will take place. It is said that good news can wait, but bad news can't.

The good news is the promise of the rapture of the church, millennial kingdom, and new heaven and new earth. We discuss that in chapter 9. The bad news is the awful tribulation that the whole world must face. Although the church can avoid the tribulation, Christians will face persecution and hardships in the near future because God has judged America. The next chapter describes the road our country has taken that has caused this time of reckoning.

4

The Root Cause

After the initial shock about the Golden Horde wears off, the citizens of Wroclaw may question whether all this defensive preparation and training is necessary. What caused the Mongols to invade in the first place? What do they want? Maybe they will quit and go home.

A leader can explain that the Mongol imperial treasury is empty, and the army is grumbling. Discontent fuels revolt. The Mongol leaders must conquer other nations to fill the treasury and keep the army loyal. So far, their invasion is working. They have won victory after victory and show no sign of quitting.

To do nothing today is not an option for Christians either. Now is not the time for apathy. Why? The world has turned upside down. Cultural acceptance of sexual sin has swamped our country with the force of a tsunami and left sexual chaos in its wake.

America was once a beacon to the world, a land that once honored God and in return was blessed. We became the richest and most powerful country in history. But nations don't stay powerful forever, not if they violate what made them great to begin with. America is no exception.

Beginning in the 1960s, America began to rot from within from sexual sin. The decay has dramatically accelerated within the last fifteen years. In this chapter we will explain the cause, which has precipitated our need to train for a coming persecution.

God made the rules for gender, sex, marriage, and the family. The United States has violated those rules and will soon pay the price.

God's Rules

Two Sexes. God created only two sexes, male and female:

> So God created mankind in his own image, in the image of God he created them; male and female he created them. (Genesis 1:27)

Procreation. God created sex for procreation:
> God blessed them and said to them, "Be fruitful and increase in number; fill the earth and subdue it. Rule

over the fish in the sea and the birds in the sky and over every living creature that moves on the ground." (Genesis 1:28)

Marriage. God created marriage as the only environment for a man and a woman to have sex and raise a family:

The man said, "This is now bone of my bones and flesh of my flesh; she shall be called 'woman,' for she was taken out of man." That is why a man leaves his father and mother and is united to his wife, and they become one flesh. (Genesis 2:23–24)

"Haven't you read," he [Jesus] replied, "that at the beginning the Creator 'made them male and female,' and said, 'For this reason a man will leave his father and mother and be united to his wife, and the two will become one flesh'? So they are no longer two, but one flesh. Therefore what God has joined together, let no one separate." (Matthew 19:4–6)

Gender Roles. God designed men and women to have different but complimentary roles:

The Lord God said, "It is not good for the man to be alone. I will make a helper suitable for him." (Genesis 2:18)

Family. God designed the nuclear family of a father and mother for children:

Listen, my son, to your father's instruction and do not forsake your mother's teaching. (Proverbs 1:8)

Research shows that children do best in a family with a father and a mother. A 2015 issue of Princeton and Brooking's *Future of Children* disclosed that:

> Whereas **most scholars now agree** that children raised
> by two biological parents in a stable marriage do better
> than children in other family forms across a wide
> range of outcomes, there is less consensus about why.
> (emphasis added)[31]

Bible believing Christians know why. It is God's created order. Furthermore, a Brookings Institution report states that societies do best with intact biblical families:

> Do states with more families headed by married parents
> enjoy greater prosperity and give poor children a better
> shot at the American Dream? The short answer: "yes."[32]

The family unit of a father, mother, and children is the foundation of society. Destroy the family, and society dissolves into chaos. That is what we face today: one-parent families, gangs, violence, poverty, suicide, drug use, etc. It all is the consequence of sexual sin.

The Curse of Sexual Sin

Why is sexual sin such a big deal? It is an assault on God's creative order. Consider the number of verses in the New Testament alone that warn against sexual sin: Matthew 15:19, Mark 7:20–23, John 8:3–11, Acts 15:29, 1 Corinthians 10:8, 2 Corinthians 12:21, Galatians 5:19, Ephesians 5:3, Colossians 3:5, 1 Thessalonians 4:3, 1 Timothy 1:10, 2 Timothy 2:22, Titus 2:12, Hebrews 13:4, James 2:11, 1 Peter 2:11, 2 Peter 2:14, 1 John 2:16, Jude 7, Revelation 21:8.

Notice the seriousness of sexual immorality, included in the following list with murder and idolatry:

> But the cowardly, the unbelieving, the vile, the
> murderers, the **sexually immoral,** those who practice
> magic arts, the idolaters and all liars—they will be
> consigned to the fiery lake of burning sulfur. This is
> the second death. (Revelation 21:8) (emphasis added)

The following are some specific biblical prohibitions against sexual immorality:

Premarital Sex. God prohibits premarital sex and created marriage as the only environment to have sex:

> But since sexual immorality is occurring, each man should have sexual relations with his own wife, and each woman with her own husband. (1 Corinthians 7:2)

Pornography. God prohibits lust:

> But I tell you that anyone who looks at a woman lustfully has already committed adultery with her in his heart. If your right eye causes you to stumble, gouge it out and throw it away. It is better for you to lose one part of your body than for your whole body to be thrown into hell." (Matthew 5:28–29)

> I made a covenant with my eyes not to look lustfully at a young woman. For what is our lot from God above, our heritage from the Almighty on high? Is it not ruin for the wicked, disaster for those who do wrong? (Job 31:1–3)

Abortion. God creates human beings at conception. To kill a baby in the womb is murder:

> If people are fighting and hit a pregnant woman and she gives birth prematurely but there is no serious injury, the offender must be fined whatever the woman's husband demands and the court allows. But if there is serious injury, you are to take life for life. (Exodus 21:22–23)

> For you created my inmost being; you knit me together in my mother's womb. (Psalm 139:13)

Homosexuality. God prohibits homosexual sex:

> If a man has sexual relations with a man as one does with a woman, both of them have done what is detestable. They are to be put to death; their blood will be on their own heads. (Leviticus 20:13)

> We know that the law is good if one uses it properly. We also know that the law is made not for the righteous but for lawbreakers and rebels, the ungodly and sinful, the unholy and irreligious, for those who kill their fathers or mothers, for murderers, for the sexually immoral, for those practicing homosexuality, for slave traders and liars and perjurers—and for whatever else is contrary to the sound doctrine that conforms to the gospel concerning the glory of the blessed God, which he entrusted to me. (1 Timothy 1:8–11).

Sexual sin began to spread like a virus with the 1960s sexual revolution. Biblical moral standards were challenged and upended. The sexual revolution sought nothing less than to erase the old sexual morals from society and impose a new sexual order. Today, a broad coalition of government, courts, media, academia, entertainment, and big corporations is forcefully imposing this new sexual order.

Progression of Sexual Sin

During the first half of the twentieth century almost all young women wanted to be married, most by age twenty-two. They desired four children and to raise them at home. Couples rarely divorced, and when they did, their reputations, both personally and professionally, were harmed. Society discouraged premarital sex, and if pregnancy resulted, parents arranged a "shotgun marriage." Society also condemned homosexuality and rarely discussed it.[33]

Then came the sexual revolution, following the development of birth control and antibiotics for syphilis. Scientists had removed two impediments to fornication: the fear of pregnancy and disease.

Radical feminists called for women to sever their dependence on men and to enjoy sex like men without the consequences. Promiscuous sex increased, but the use of birth control did not decrease unwanted pregnancies or abortions. Rather, out of wedlock births increased because shotgun weddings became a thing of the past. Abortions increased dramatically as well.

The increase in the supply of women willing to have sex without any commitment from men to marry eliminated women's leverage. Men got what they wanted without giving up anything in return. Consequently, single parent households surged, forcing women to both nurture the children and assume the husband's role as provider.

Feminism. Betty Friedan (1921–2006) launched the second wave of feminism. The first wave was women's suffrage. The second wave encouraged women to seek careers outside of the home, overcoming their "subordination to male privilege." Her book *The Feminine Mystique*, published in 1963, challenged the notion that women were fulfilled by staying at home and raising children. She compared suburban housewives to concentration camp victims and women who made themselves beautiful to pitiful sex seekers.

Friedan, a Marxist and humanist, claimed that women had an identity crisis. The solution? Women must pursue creative work in a career, not by creating a home and family. To that end, she promoted no-fault divorce, birth control, abortion, elimination of sex discrimination, government childcare, and a gender-neutral society.

Radical feminists strive for sexual equality with men, viewing children as a burden and marriage as a form of slavery. If men can have sex without bearing children, why can't women? Birth control and abortion grant equality to women by freeing them from bearing children[34] and allow them to have sex like men.

Birth Control. Margaret Sanger (1879–1966), a sexually promiscuous "free thinker," was a pioneering birth control activist and writer, who in 1916 opened the first birth control clinic in the United States. In 1921 she founded the American Birth Control League, which later became Planned Parenthood.

Sanger was a eugenicist (science of controlling human breeding to improve the race). Influenced by Darwin, she wrote,

The lower down in the scale of human development we go the less sexual control we find. It is said the aboriginal Australian, the lowest known species of the human family, just a step higher than the chimpanzee in brain development, has so little sexual control that police authority alone prevents him from obtaining sexual satisfaction on the streets.[35]

Sanger saw her dream fulfilled when the *Griswold v. Connecticut* (1965) Supreme Court case overturned an 1879 state law prohibiting the use of drugs or devices to prevent conception, a law that was originally designed to promote stable families by discouraging adultery. The Connecticut law was similar to laws passed in thirty other states and upheld by state supreme courts over many years.

Justice William O. Douglas defended the Griswold ruling, despite zero support in the Constitution, with a verbal sleight of hand, using terms such as "penumbras" (shadows), "emanations," and "zones of privacy."

In his majority opinion he wrote, "specific guarantees in the Bill of Rights have penumbras, formed by emanations from those guarantees that help give them life and substance" and "various of these guarantees create zones of privacy"[36] that cannot be infringed. Seven years later, *Eisenstadt v. Baird* (1972) struck down a Massachusetts law prohibiting the distribution of contraceptives to unmarried people.

Abortion. Although Margaret Sanger resigned from the American Birth Control League in 1928, it grew to be the most powerful eugenics organization in the world. Because the Nazis were associated with eugenics during World War II and killed six million Jews, the American Birth Control League changed its name to Planned Parenthood.

In 1969 Dr. Bernard Nathanson (1926 – 2011), an obstetrician/gynecologist in New York City, joined Lawrence Lake and Betty Friedan to form the National Association for the Repeal of Abortion Laws (NARAL, now called NARAL Pro-Choice America), the country's largest abortion lobby.

As reported in David Kupelian's book, *The Marketing of Evil,* Nathanson explained how they reversed public opinion about abortion.

They rebranded abortion from feticide to "women's rights," by creating slogans, such as "freedom of choice" and "women must have control over their own bodies." Nathanson recalls, "I remember laughing when we made those slogans up. We were looking for some sexy, catchy slogans to capture public opinion. They were very cynical slogans then, just as all of these slogans today are very, very cynical."[37]

They fed the media lies, grossly inflating the number of illegal abortions performed and the deaths that resulted. They consistently claimed that one million illegal abortions were performed annually, when the actual figure was ten times less, 100,000. They also claimed that 10,000 annual deaths resulted, when the real figure was 200–250. They said that the number of abortions wouldn't go up; that the illegal abortions would merely become legal. In reality, abortions have become a primary birth control method and have risen dramatically.[37] Their goal was achieved with the *Roe v. Wade* (1973) Supreme Court decision.

As chief of obstetrical services at St. Luke's Hospital in New York City, Nathanson switched sides on the abortion issue and became a pro-life advocate after viewing a newly acquired ultrasound machine demonstration. In 1984 he videotaped the ultrasound of a woman undergoing an abortion after three months of pregnancy. It was a shattering experience. The baby tried to wiggle away from the suction device. The tiny figure continued to struggle even after he was severely maimed. Then, he opened his mouth as if to scream. From that video Nathanson made a 28-minute documentary called *The Silent Scream*.

Since 1973 over 60 million children have been aborted in the United States[38]

Birth rate below replacement rate. The consequence of birth control and abortion is that the birth rate has declined in the West below the replacement rate. According to a *U.S. News & World Report* article, "American women are now projected to have about 1.71 children over their lifetimes … below the rate of 2.1 needed to exactly replace a generation." The fertility rate has fallen below the replacement rate since 1971.[39] In the West, "be fruitful and multiply" is practiced by too few people.

Divorce. Before the 1960s, most of the population shared the same attitudes about marriage, family, and sex. Adultery was shameful, and divorce rare. A man was expected to marry a pregnant girlfriend and provide financial support.

In 1960 the number of divorces per year among 1,000 married women in the United States was 9.2. After no-fault divorce was first enacted in 1969, the divorce rate jumped to 22.6 in 1980 and declined to 17.5 in 2007, still nearly twice the divorce rate in 1960.[40] Two-thirds of divorces are initiated by women.[41]

One reason the divorce rate declined since 1980 is that fewer people are marrying; they are cohabiting instead. Since 1950, the marriage rate has declined by two-thirds, dropping from 90.2 marriages per 1,000 unmarried women in 1950 to 31.1 in 2011.[42]

Since the marriage rate has declined, the birth rate for unmarried women has exploded from 5.3 percent in 1960 to 40.3 percent in 2014.[43]

Legalization of Sodomy. In 1960, sodomy was a crime in all fifty states. The road to legalization began with the "science" of now discredited Indiana University professor Alfred Kinsey (1894 – 1956), and his two influential books: the *Sexual Behavior in the Human Male* (1948) and *Sexual Behavior in the Human Female* (1953).

Kinsey claimed that 10 percent to 47 percent of Americans were to some degree homosexual. The 10 percent number was important. After all, blacks were 10 percent of the population in 1950, and 10 percent made homosexuals a sufficiently large minority class.[44]

The problem, as it turns out, was that Kinsey's convincing figures were all wrong. Gallup has shown that the American public grossly overestimates the size of the homosexual population. Eighty-seven percent of the American public think that more than 10 percent of the population is homosexual, and a whopping 54 percent think that more than 20 percent of the population is homosexual. Only a paltry 8 percent know the truth[45] that only 2 percent of the population is homosexual.

Kinsey drew his statistical sample pool from active child molesters, incarcerated sex offenders, pimps, male prostitutes, and homosexual activists at gay bars; none of whom were representative of the general male population. Kinsey was hardly a neutral researcher. He participated in his own sexual experiments filmed in his attic and was a sadomasochistic bisexual who had homosexual affairs.[46] However, Kinsey's stock is still high in academia and the LGBTQ community, as is his so-called

Kinsey Scale that purports to measure sexuality on a continuum from 0, exclusively heterosexual, to 6, exclusively homosexual.[44]

Kinsey would have been pleased that the Supreme Court in the 2003 *Lawrence v. Texas* case legalized sodomy, overturning a Texas law that was rarely enforced. In fact, the state admitted in 1994 that it had not prosecuted anyone as of that date.[47]

According to the book *Flagrant Conduct* by University of Minnesota professor Dale Carpenter, in September 1998 a homosexual "couple" (one white and the other black) visited another homosexual man's apartment and began drinking heavily. An argument arose when the visitor's lover began to flirt with the apartment's occupant. The jealous man stormed out, and called the police, alleging that "a black male [was] going crazy with a gun." After entering the unlocked apartment, the lead officer claimed that the two men were engaged in homosexual sex.

Gay legal activists packaged the case as a love story, just two committed men cementing a bond through lovemaking, and the case eventually made it to the Supreme Court. In his majority opinion, Justice Anthony Kennedy wrote, "when sexuality finds overt expression in intimate conduct with another person, the conduct can be but one element in a personal bond that is more enduring."[48] In the majority opinion, the justices denied their decision would lead to legalizing same-sex marriage, but dissenting Judge Antonin Scalia wrote, "Don't believe it."[49]

Homosexual Marriage. In fact, the legalization of sodomy did lead to the legalization of homosexual marriage. The story is a case study of how the Left has overturned the biblical morals of an entire society. After all, only about 2 percent of the population is homosexual. How can a practice that 98 percent of the population once found revolting now seem normal? After all, the human waste processing channel is not a sexual organ.

No public opinion attitude in the United States has changed more quickly than that regarding same-sex marriage.[50] The attitudes about homosexual marriage from 1996, when the Defense of Marriage Act was signed into law, to 2020 have flipped. In 1996 68 percent of the public opposed homosexual marriage. Today, 67 percent of the public *supports* it.

War Conference. The campaign to normalize homosexuality began at a 1988 war conference of 175 leading gay activists, who met in Warrenton, Virginia. They planned a public relations and propaganda campaign to force the public to accept the homosexual culture and to silence the opposition. Their objective was to desensitize homosexuality by deluging the public with pro-homosexual messages, positive images, and sympathetic news. The continuous drumbeat of messages would cause the public to eventually shrug its shoulders about homosexuality.[51]

Playbook. In 1989 a book by Marshal Kirk and Hunter Madsen (under the pen name Erastes Pill), titled *After the Ball—How America Will Conquer Its Fear and Hatred of Gays in the 90s,* was published. The book was a more extensive treatment of an article written two years earlier in *Guide* magazine titled "The Overhauling of Straight America." About the book, noted theologian Albert Mohler wrote,

> A partial explanation of the homosexual movement's success can be traced to the 1989 publication of *After the Ball: How America Will Conquer Its Fear and Hatred of Gays in the 90s.* Published with little fanfare, this book became the authoritative public relations manual for the homosexual agenda, and its authors presented the book as a distillation of public relations advice for the homosexual community.[52]

Both the article and book lay out a surprisingly frank blueprint to get the public, without their awareness, to move from revulsion of homosexuality to *approval* of homosexuality.

Both Kirk and Madsen were Harvard educated. Kirk was a researcher in neuropsychiatry, and Madsen was a social scientist and public relations consultant. They cleverly devised sophisticated psychological techniques to persuade the public that homosexuality was normal. In the words of *After the Ball*, "We mean conversion of the average American's emotions, mind, and will, through a planned psychological attack in the form of propaganda fed to the nation via the media."[53] The propaganda campaign prescribed the following:

1. "Talk about gays and gayness as loudly and as often as possible." Force the public to eventually tire of the issue and become desensitized.
2. "Portray gays as victims, not as aggressive challengers." Exploit the Matthew Shepard murder case and demonize Christian leaders as homophobes.
3. "Give homosexual protectors a just cause." Repeat slogans such as "the fight for gay rights," "gay pride," and "respect and dignity of gay people."
4. "Make gays look good." Never portray real-life homosexuals, such as the "mustachioed leather-man, drag queens, and bull dykes"; how the sex is actually performed; the hundreds of sex partners; the sadomasochistic practices; or the sex with juveniles. Claim that many historical figures were homosexuals, despite a lack of evidence.
5. "Make the victimizers look bad." Portray conservative Christian pastors as "hysterical backwoods preachers, drooling with hate to a degree that looks both comical and deranged." Induce liberal churches to claim that the Bible does not condemn homosexual behavior.

The entertainment industry has followed the playbook in a big way.

Influential Gay TV Shows. An October 18, 2000, episode of *The West Wing* is a good illustration of how the media portray homosexuals as victims and those who oppose homosexuality as narrow-minded homophobes. The president, played by Martin Sheen, shames a radio talk show host character, Dr. Jenna Jacobs, about the anti-homosexual advice she gives on her radio program, including her contention that homosexuality is an abomination, citing Leviticus in the Bible. The Jacobs character was a thinly veiled portrayal of real-life marriage therapist Dr. Laura Schlessinger, whose TV show gay activists were trying to cancel—and eventually succeeded—because she deemed homosexuality to be a disorder.

The president dresses down Dr. Jacobs and mockingly asks if he should sell his daughter into slavery as Exodus 21:7 allows, or kill his colleague for working on the Sabbath as Exodus 20 prescribes, or forbid the Washington Redskins from playing football because they must touch the skin of a pig outlawed by Deuteronomy 14:8. Poor Dr. Jacobs must stare at the floor, exposed as a prejudiced posturer. The superior presidential figure has righteously savaged her. He uses the familiar, "you're just cherry-picking verses but ignoring others" ploy but conveniently ignores the moral and ceremonial law distinctions of the Old Testament laws and the general and specific distinctions of applying the laws to the world as a whole and Israel in particular.

Other shows, which favorably portrayed homosexuals, include *Will & Grace* (1998 to 2006), *Glee* (2009–2015), *Queer Eye for the Straight Guy* (2003–2007); and even *Arthur*, during its 2019 premiere. GLAAD (formerly called the Gay & Lesbian Alliance Against Defamation) discloses in their yearly report *Where Are We on TV* that LGBT characters on primetime TV have increased ten-fold since 2005, from ten LGBT characters in 2005, representing around 1% of all the characters, to ninety in 2019, representing over 10 percent of the total.

Corporations are also following the playbook. The Human Rights Campaign (HRC), founded in 1980, is the largest LGBTQ lobbying organization in the United States. It publishes a so-called Corporate Equality Index, in which it rates companies on "their commitment to LGBTQ equality and inclusion." It reports that 214 of the Fortune 500 companies received a one-hundred-percent rating, which includes "public commitment to the LGBTQ community."[54]

Influential Gay Movies. Hollywood follows the playbook as well. A watershed movie was *Philadelphia* (1997), which portrayed a homosexual character as a victim and those opposed to homosexuality as bigots.

The late clinical professor of psychiatry Dr. Charles Socarides explained how *Philadelphia* employed elements of the *After the Ball* strategy,

> In the movie "Philadelphia" we see the shaming technique and the conversion process working at the highest media level. We saw Tom Hank's character suffering (because he was gay and had AIDS) at the hands of bigots in his Philadelphia law firm. Not only

were we ashamed of the homophobic behavior of the villainous straight lawyers in the firm; we felt nothing but sympathy for the suffering Hanks. (Members of the Motion Picture Academy felt so much sympathy they gave Hanks an Oscar.)[55]

Throughout American history, until the last half of the twentieth century, homosexuality was considered aberrant behavior and a mental disorder by the American Psychiatric Association (APA).

Declassification as a Mental Disorder. To normalize homosexual behavior, homosexual activists mounted an aggressive campaign to convince the APA to change their *Diagnostic and Statistical Manual of Mental Disorders* (DSM). The following chart shows the gradual disappearance of homosexuality as a disorder from the DSM.

The Curious Disappearance of Homosexuality
as a Mental Disorder from the DSM

Edition	Date	Homosexual Reference
1st	1952	"Sociopathic personality disorder"
2nd	1968	"Sexual deviation"
3rd	1980	Feeling distressed about homosexual feelings is a disorder, not being a homosexual
4th	1987	Deleted entirely

Activists began disrupting APA meetings and conferences that contested the homosexual cause. According to Socarides:

> In 1972 and 1973 they [gay lobby] co-opted the leadership of the American Psychiatric Association through a series of political maneuvers, lies and outright flim-flam, they 'cured' homosexuality overnight by fiat. They got the APA to say that same-sex sex was 'not a disorder.' It was merely 'a condition'—as neutral as left handedness.[55]

Activists focused their attention on New York psychiatrist Robert

Spitzer, the chair of the APA's task force for the third edition of the DSM. An atheist who was married three times, Spitzer was pressured by gay activists to remove homosexuality as a form of mental illness. Spitzer complied by establishing a new category called sexual orientation disturbance. Homosexuality was removed and sexual orientation disturbance added so psychiatrists could retain their business treating people disturbed by same-sex attraction.

A mass mailing was sent to the 30,000 APA members by a pro-homosexual faction, purportedly funded by the National Gay Task Force, that encouraged all members to agree to the change. Only one-third responded, but the measure passed.[51] This was not really the voice of practicing psychiatrists, however. Four years later, the results of a survey of 2,500 psychiatrists revealed that 69 percent considered homosexuality to be a pathological disorder, not normal behavior.[44] However, the damage was done, and later the American Psychological Association followed suit.

Frame the Issues as a Positive Good. The Left discovered a final winning formula to win over the public to homosexual marriage. The "godfather" of the homosexual marriage movement was Even Wolfson, a Harvard Law School educated lawyer. After working for twelve years at Lambda Legal, the nation's largest LGBTQ advocacy law firm, as the director of their Marriage Project, Wolfson left to form the organization Freedom to Marry, helped by a $2.5 million grant by the Evelyn & Walter Haas Jr. Fund. In 2005 Wolfson and others created the "2020 Vision to legalize gay marriage."

The group conducted cutting-edge qualitative research, complete with focus groups, to discover a message that would deceive middle American voters to support homosexual marriage. Their researchers found that arguing for the rights of homosexuals to marry was not convincing. But, when they portrayed homosexual marriage as "loving" and "committed," just like traditional marriages and that homosexual couples wanted to marry for the same reasons as a man and women would, well, that resonated with middle America.[56]

How could heterosexuals deny homosexuals the opportunity to form a "committed union"? How could heterosexuals deny homosexuals the freedom to love? Didn't Jesus say to do unto others as you would have them do unto you?

Ted Olson, George W. Bush's Solicitor General, who later argued the case before the Supreme Court that overturned Proposition 8, a California law that protected traditional marriage and outlawed homosexual marriage, echoed Wolfson's message in a National Public Radio *Talk of the Nation* interview, "… how could you be against a relationship in which people who *love* one another … and engage in a household in which they are *committed* to one another …"[57] Joe Biden over the years when asked about his loyalty to the LGBTQ cause predictably trots out a far-fetched story about he and his father *in the 1950s.* The two supposedly witnessed two men kissing each other in public and the father explains to his son, "Joey, they *love* each other."

Obergefell Decision. The homosexual propaganda campaign paid off with the 2015 *Obergefell v. Hodges* Supreme Court case that legalized gay marriage. The 5–4 decision required all states to issue marriage licenses to same-sex couples and to recognize same-sex marriages performed in other states. Responding to the opinion, the Obama White House was bathed in rainbow colors and the Department of the Interior tweeted a picture of two men kissing passionately.[58]

The *Obergefell v. Hodges* dissent by the Supreme Court minority justices was unusually harsh and dismissive. Chief Justice of the United States John Roberts, joined by Justices Scalia and Thomas, wrote that the traditional meaning of marriage has existed "throughout human history." Roberts warned that,

> Five lawyers have closed the debate and enacted their own vision of marriage as a matter of constitutional law. Stealing this issue from the people will for many cast a cloud over same-sex marriage, making a dramatic social change that much more difficult to accept. The majority's decision is an act of will, not legal judgment. The right it announces has no basis in the Constitution or this Court's precedent … [The court has transformed] a social institution that has formed the basis of human society for millennia, for the Kalahari Bushmen and the Han

Chinese, the Carthaginians and the Aztecs. Just who do we think we are? … Today's decision, for example, creates serious questions about religious liberty.[59]

Those questions were answered in 2018, when the House of Representatives voted to pass the grotesquely misnamed Equal Rights Act that would discriminate against Christian's religious consciences regarding homosexuality and transgenderism. The vote: Democrats 228 Ayes and 0 Noes. Republicans 8 Ayes and 173 Noes.

Ironically, the godless communist countries of the Cold War era, Russia and China, are godlier than the Christian West. Neither Russia nor China allow same-sex marriage. Meanwhile, we have a transportation secretary, Pete Buttigieg, in the Biden administration, who is "married" to a man. Our Army has run an ad with a corporal who proudly discloses she was raised by two lesbian women married to each other. Likewise, a CIA ad featured an agent who discloses he is gay.

Transgenderism. The most recent progression of sexual sin is the transgender movement, where the propaganda techniques that made homosexuality mainstream and normal are reused.

Popular films such as the Oscar-winning *Boys Don't Cry*, *The Crying Game*, and *Normal* portray transsexuals as victims of prejudice, not as cognitively and emotionally confused.

Television characters such as the transsexual in the highly popular *Ugly Betty* program use the likeability factor to overcome society's aversion to one sex acting like the opposite sex.

Sympathetic journalism doesn't get any better than in 2007 when Barbara Walters in the *20/20* episode, "My Secret Self," invited viewers to "open [their] hearts and minds" to "courageous and loving parents" who allowed their transsexual children to live as the opposite sex, promising, "most of you will be moved" by their stories.[60]

As gay activists did in 1973, transsexual advocates today are pressuring the American Psychiatric Association to revise its *Diagnostic and Statistical Manual* to eliminate transsexualism (or gender identity disorder) as a classifiable disorder.[60] Today, a former men's Olympic decathlon gold medalist, who claims he is a woman, is celebrated as a hero.

Educational reforms that name transsexuals as a protected class have swept through high school and college campuses, as well as corporations and the government.[60] In 2019 two teenaged biological male sprinters, who claimed they were females, placed one and two in the girl's state high school track championships in Connecticut. In 2021 a University of Pennsylvania swimmer, formerly named Will Thomas, an average swimmer on the men's team for two years, now sets records on the women's team as Lia Thomas.

The administration promoted a four-star admiral, Rachel Levine, a "transwoman," formerly known as Richard, to be the Assistant Secretary for Health and head of the U.S. Public Health Service. Our State Department celebrated International Pronouns Day, a day after Levine's promotion. Now, people expect us to refer to an *individual* as "they," not he or she, if that individual is sexually "neutral."

The final effect of this steady drumbeat of propaganda over the years is revealed by the startling results of a survey[61] conducted by Arizona Christian University. They report that about *39 percent* of 18 to 24-year-olds (Gen Z) identify as LGBTQ. Whether these Gen Z-ers actually *are* LGBTQ is highly suspect. What is not suspect is that these young people have been brainwashed and influenced by peer pressure to virtue signal by identifying with an approved group.

Conclusion

Support for homosexual marriage in the United States flipped in thirty years. Within the last ten years transgenderism has gained massive support from the cultural elites and is also becoming mainstream. Plus, a soft totalitarianism is creeping into government, industry, and education coercing acceptance of the new sexual order (more about that in chapter 6). Any attempt to roll back the gains of abortionists, homosexuals, and transsexuals will meet with vicious resistance.

Since sex is meaningless, marriage is meaningless, gender is meaningless, and so is the family. Is it any wonder that the world seems upside down? That's because it is.

Our country has turned from God, and God has turned from us. We will discuss that next.

5

The Threat

The citizens of Wroclaw now understand that the Golden Horde will not quit unless defeated. However, some citizens may question the severity of the threat. What could happen to the city? How bad could it actually be? Everything seems so normal now.

A leader would explain that the Mongols kill, rape, and plunder when they invade. The enemy shows no pity. Work on the defenses must continue because the threat is dire indeed.

To train for the end times, we also must be convinced that the threat is serious enough to justify the time and effort to train. Life may seem normal now. After all, there is no fire and brimstone falling from the sky. You may think this end times talk is overblown. However, don't let up. You must understand how rapidly our country has declined and how seriously God has judged us.

So, where is America in end-times prophecy? The short answer is that it is ominously absent. According to noted pastor and prophecy scholar Dr. David Jeremiah, "Indeed, no specific mention of the United States or any other country in North or South America can be found in the Bible."[62]

That is dire. How can Israel's most powerful ally be absent during the Ezekiel 38 and 39 Russian-Muslim coalition's invasion of Israel? According to Dr. Jeremiah, there are five possible explanations: America may have joined the Antichrist's ten nation coalition; America may lose its sovereignty due to financial insolvency and be absorbed into the new world order; America may be invaded by outside forces; America may be incapacitated by the rapture and disappearance of Christians; or America may rot from within from moral decay.[63]

We believe the latter has occurred, and America is under judgment today. We also believe that God's punishment will ratchet up because moral decay from sexual sin has accelerated. Perhaps a natural disaster, such as an earthquake, will trigger an economic collapse. Of course, we could be wrong, but we will build our case in this chapter.

Will God Punish Our Country for Sexual Sin?

Many prominent theologians have warned that God will punish our country for sexual sin, including John MacArthur, Franklin Graham, John Hagee, Robert Jeffress, and Pat Robertson.

John MacArthur. Pastor John F. MacArthur delivered a sermon titled "When God Abandons a Nation,"[64] at his Grace Community Church in Sun Valley, California, on Sunday, August 20, 2006, in which he described three stages of abandonment found in Romans 1:18–32 that apply to America. God has abandoned America, because America has abandoned God. As His restraining grace is removed, the country sinks into ever grosser immorality.

Why has God abandoned America?

People deep down know there is a God. It is obvious by observing the beauty, diversity, and complexity of life. Nevertheless, people do not glorify or give thanks to God.

> The wrath of God is being revealed from heaven against all the godlessness and wickedness of people, who suppress the truth by their wickedness, since what may be known about God is plain to them, because God has made it plain to them. For since the creation of the world God's invisible qualities—his eternal power and divine nature—have been clearly seen, being understood from what has been made, so that people are without excuse. (Romans 1:18–20)

People deny that God created the universe. They have replaced God with evolution. They say man is the product of random mutations over billions of years and conclude that God did not create man or make him in God's image.

> For although they knew God, they neither glorified him as God nor gave thanks to him, but their thinking became futile and their foolish hearts were darkened. Although they claimed to be wise, they became fools and exchanged the glory of the immortal God for

images made to look like a mortal human being and birds and animals and reptiles … They exchanged the truth about God for a lie, and worshiped and served created things rather than the Creator—who is forever praised. Amen. (Romans 1:21–23, 25)

This is manifest in the religion of environmentalism. On September 15, 2003, the late writer Michael Crichton gave a talk titled, "Environmentalism Is a Religion" at the Commonwealth Club in San Francisco. Crichton, author of *Jurassic Park* and many other popular books and by no means an evangelical Christian, stated the following:

Today, one of the most powerful religions in the Western World is environmentalism. Environmentalism seems to be the religion of choice for urban atheists. Why do I say it's a religion? Well, just look at the beliefs. If you look carefully, you see that environmentalism is in fact a perfect 21st century remapping of traditional Judeo-Christian beliefs and myths. There's an initial Eden, a paradise, a state of grace and unity with nature, there's a fall from grace into a state of pollution as a result of eating from the tree of knowledge, and as a result of our actions there is a judgment day coming for us all. We are all energy sinners, doomed to die, unless we seek salvation, which is now called sustainability. Sustainability is salvation in the church of the environment. Just as organic food is its communion, that pesticide-free wafer that the right people with the right beliefs, imbibe.

Eden, the fall of man, the loss of grace, the coming doomsday—these are deeply held mythic structures.[65]

Since the MacArthur sermon, the religion of environmentalism has progressed.

- Beginning in 2013, over a three-and-a-half-year period, a New York lawyer argued that the court should grant two chimpanzees named Kiko and Tommy the same legal rights as humans.[66]
- In a January 2019 speech, Representative Alexandria Ocasio-Cortez of New York claimed "The world is going to end in 12 years if we don't address climate change,"[67] basing her remarks on a 2018 report by the U.N. Intergovernmental Panel on Climate Change.
- In February 2019, Ocasio-Cortez suggested it would not be ethical to have children because of the effects of climate change.[68]
- In September 2019, students at Union Theological Seminary in a chapel service confessed their environmental sins to plants.[69]
- In December 2019, a mayoral candidate in Clearwater, Florida, claimed that "Natural wonders should have their own legal rights,"[70] referring to rivers, mountains, meadows, lakes, trees, etc.

In addition to environmentalism, MacArthur in his sermon also noted that American society has turned away from God by declaring truth is relative, people are basically good and can control who they become, and the goal of life is self-satisfaction.

The evidence that God has abandoned America is revealed in the Romans 1 passage by the words, "God gave them over." MacArthur explains that this has occurred in three stages during the country's recent history.

Stage 1: Rampant Sexual Immorality

> Therefore God gave them over in the sinful desires of their hearts to sexual impurity for the degrading of their bodies with one another. (Romans 1:24)

Sexual immorality is everywhere in America. We are the world's leading exporter of pornography. The Pew Research Center reports that "78% of those ages 18 to 29 say it's acceptable for an unmarried couple to live together, even if they don't plan to get married."[71] We have aborted over sixty million babies. Pew Research also reports, "Almost a quarter of U.S. children under the age of 18 live with one parent and no other adults (23%), more than three times the share of children around the world who do so (7%)."[72]

Stage 2: Sexual Degradation, Manifested by Homosexuality

> Because of this, God gave them over to shameful lusts. Even their women exchanged natural sexual relations for unnatural ones. In the same way the men also abandoned natural relations with women and were inflamed with lust for one another. Men committed shameful acts with other men, and received in themselves the due penalty for their error. (Romans 1:26–27)

The degradation of women, lesbianism, usually occurs last in a nation's sinful progression, because women naturally desire to bear and nurture children. Homosexuals have "received in themselves the due penalty for their error" through sexually transmitted diseases, particularly AIDS.

Stage 3: Depravity

> Furthermore, just as they did not think it worthwhile to retain the knowledge of God, so God gave them over to a depraved mind, so that they do what ought not to be done. They have become filled with every kind of wickedness, evil, greed and depravity. They are full of envy, murder, strife, deceit and malice. They are gossips, slanderers, God-haters, insolent, arrogant and boastful; they invent ways of doing evil; they disobey their parents; they have no understanding, no fidelity, no love, no mercy. (Romans 1:28–31)

We witness all those depraved characteristics today: the wickedness and evil of sexual sin; the greed of Bernie Madoff; the depravity of homosexual and lesbian sex; the envy of socialism; the murder through mass killings, school shootings, and abortion; the strife of a divided Congress and country and rioting in the cities; the deceit, malice, gossip, and slander of fake news on TV and the internet; the haters of God who censor Christian views in the public square; the insolence, arrogance, and boastfulness of our political leaders; and the inventors of evil with their notion that gender is fluid and changeable and people are no longer reliably identified as male or female at birth.

The final manifestation of the third stage occurs when the cultural elites not only commit these ungodly acts, but approve of those who practice them. Consider all the prominent celebrities, newscasters, and sports figures who applaud abortion, homosexuality, and transgenderism.

> Although they know God's righteous decree that those who do such things deserve death, they not only continue to do these very things but also approve of those who practice them. (Romans 1:32)

Therefore, the evidence reveals that God has abandoned us.
Franklin Graham. In 2012, Franklin Graham wrote,

> After watching the political conventions of both parties last month, it's clear that America is quickly hurtling down a road toward God's judgment.

> One party affirms a belief in the sanctity of life. The other party does not. One party supports the traditional, biblical definition of marriage between one man and one woman. The other party enthusiastically endorses and promotes same-sex marriage.

> I will not—cannot—vote for a candidate, regardless of their political affiliation, who supports same-sex marriage and advocates abortion. **God will judge our nation if we continue down this path.** (emphasis added)[73]

After President Obama claimed the 2015 Obergefell Supreme Court ruling was a "victory for America," Graham stated, "God will judge him and us as a nation if we don't repent."[74]

John Hagee. Likewise, in 2015 John Hagee, founder and senior pastor of Cornerstone Church in San Antonio, declared; "This Supreme Court has made American the new Sodom and Gomorrah. God will have to judge America or He's going to have to apologize to Sodom and Gomorrah."[75]

Robert Jeffress. At a Sunday service in 2017, Robert Jeffress, senior pastor of First Baptist Church in Dallas, said, "Unless there is a great spiritual revival, America's collapse is inevitable."[76]

Pat Robertson. In 2019, regarding the Democrat's proposed Equality Act, televangelist Pat Robertson warned:

> If you want to bring the judgment of God on this nation, you just keep this stuff up. You know, I was reading in Leviticus, where it says "because of these things, the land will vomit you out." Vomit you out. I think God will say, "I've had it with America. If you do this kind of stuff, I'm going to get rid of you as a nation."[77]

Sexual sin desecrates God's creation. He created the two sexes, male and female, to participate in the act of creation. God set sexual intercourse apart in marriage and therefore made it holy, an act designed to create human beings in the image of God. To claim that two men or two women can marry, that a man is a woman or a woman is a man, that sex outside of marriage is permissible, defiles holy creation. Some so-called Christians commit heresy when they use the Bible, God's holy word, to support homosexuality and transgenderism, pervert God's created order, and lead people astray.

Our country exports homosexuality worldwide and profanes the rainbow, the holy sign that God designated for His covenant with man to never again destroy life with the waters of a flood. With their rainbow flag, homosexual activists stole and corrupted the holy sign of God. Our State Department coerces other countries to normalize same-sex marriage and advance the LGBT agenda, partly through the creation by the Obama administration and then Secretary of State Hillary Clinton of a Special Envoy for LGBT Rights in 2015. The first envoy was an openly gay career foreign service officer named Randy Berry, who is now the US Ambassador to Nepal. In June 2021 the State Department proudly flew the LGBTQ+ flag at the embassy in Kabul, Afghanistan. Two months later Kabul was overrun by the Taliban and the embassy abandoned.

Possible Judgments Today

How might God judge us? In fact, He already has, as John MacArthur and the late David Wilkerson, author, pastor, and founder of Teen Challenge and Times Square Church in New York City, have observed.

David Wilkerson. On June 18, 1989, David Wilkerson delivered a sermon at Times Square Church titled "The Last Days of America."[78] According to Wilkerson, warnings and punishments come in increasingly severe cycles until a country is no longer redeemable. *Back then*, he was convinced that the United States had advanced to the irredeemable state.

The evidence, he revealed, is found in Deuteronomy 28, where God warns Moses and the Israelites how He will curse them for disobedience. Notice the eerie similarities to the United States.

Anarchy in cities:

Deuteronomy 28:16	*Application to United States*
"You will be cursed in the city and cursed in the country"	Our large cities experienced anarchy in the 1960s with riots and more recently in 2020 with riots over alleged police racism.

Recessions and stock market crashes:

Deuteronomy 28:17	*Application to United States*
"Your basket and your kneading trough will be cursed"	We have experienced several serious recessions and stock market plunges in 2008 and again in 2020.

Confused foreign policy:

Deuteronomy 28:19–20

"You will be cursed when you come in and cursed when you go out. The Lord will send on you curses, confusion and rebuke in everything you put your hand to, until you are destroyed and come to sudden ruin because of the evil you have done in forsaking him."

Application to United States

We negotiated a peace in Vietnam, withdrew, and the Communists overran the country. We freed up billions of dollars for the Iranians, backed by their worthless promise to stop their nuclear development, but minus any meaningful way to monitor it. We withdrew from Afghanistan in 2021, and the Taliban overran the country.

Disease:

Deuteronomy 28:21–22, 27

"The Lord will plague you with diseases until he has destroyed you from the land you are entering to possess. The Lord will strike you with wasting disease, with fever and inflammation, with scorching heat and drought, with blight and mildew, which will plague you until you perish … The Lord will afflict you with the boils of Egypt and with tumors, festering sores and the itch, from which you cannot be cured."

Application to United States

In 2020 we suffered more deaths from COVID-19 than any other country in the world. We are afflicted by HIV and AIDS with 70 percent of the cases caused by homosexual sex. The boils of Egypt, tumors, and festering sores are similar to the purple lesions and cancer caused by AIDS.

Draught:

Deuteronomy 28:24

"The Lord will turn the rain of your country into dust and powder; it will come down from the skies until you are destroyed."

Application to United States

Draught in the western United States has caused massive wildfires. Wildfires in the western United States today are three times larger than fires in the 1970s, burning six times more area, and the consequence of a wildfire season lasting seventy-eight days longer.[79]

Defeat by weaker enemies:

Deuteronomy 28:25

"The Lord will cause you to be defeated before your enemies. You will come at them from one direction but flee from them in seven, and you will become a thing of horror to all the kingdoms on earth."

Application to United States

Insignificant enemies defeat us. We were attacked on September 11, 2001, by men whose leaders hid in caves, and we have spent billions in defense since then. We left Vietnam, Iraq, and Afghanistan, surrendering the countries to our enemies, none of whom are as strong as the United States.

Broken families:

Deuteronomy 28:30

"You will be pledged to be married to a woman, but another will take her and rape her. You will build a house, but you will not live in it. You will plant a vineyard, but you will not even begin to enjoy its fruit."

Application to United States

Our homes are broken. Next to the Maldives and Belarus, the United States leads the world with the highest divorce rate.[80] The United States has the world's highest rate of children living in single-parent households, three times the world rate.[72]

Widespread bankruptcies:

Deuteronomy 28:31

"Your ox will be slaughtered before your eyes, but you will eat none of it. Your donkey will be forcibly taken from you and will not be returned. Your sheep will be given to your enemies, and no one will rescue them."

Application to United States

We have suffered waves of bankruptcies, culminating in the 2020 shutdown of our entire national economy because of COVID-19. In 2008 there were massive bankruptcies triggered by a real estate crash.

Loss of our youth:

Deuteronomy 28:32

"Your sons and daughters will be given to another nation, and you will wear out your eyes watching for them day after day, powerless to lift a hand."

Application to United States

Our youth are abandoning the Christian faith. Forty percent of millennials describe themselves as "nones," with no religious affiliation.[81]

Crippling debt:

Deuteronomy 28:43–44

"The foreigners who reside among you will rise above you higher and higher, but you will sink lower and lower. They will lend to you, but you will not lend to them. They will be the head, but you will be the tail."

Application to United States

We are a debtor nation now, borrowing from other nations. Our national debt is greater than any other country in the world and has grown to a record $29 trillion. Our debt as a percentage of GDP trails only Japan.

Judgments become progressively more serious. Here are a few possibilities:

Financial Collapse. The US may collapse financially and default on its debt. Perhaps, hyperinflation will cause prices to rise dramatically. According to the US Debt Clock, the national debt of the United States is $28.7 trillion at August 2021. A rise in interest rates on the debt would cause a catastrophe. The yearly tax revenue of the country is about $3.5 trillion. The yearly interest on the debt is $375 billion at an average interest rate of 2.2 percent. If rates rise to 5 percent, the country would have to pay around $850 billion for interest on the debt, around one-quarter of the yearly revenue of the country. Between 1965 and 1985 interest rates on ten-year Treasury bonds climbed from 4 percent to 15 percent. Any similar movement in the next twenty years could bankrupt us.

Pandemics. The world may face another pandemic, but one much more deadly than the 0.5 percent death rate of COVID-19. For example, Ebola had a death rate of 25 percent to 90 percent but mercifully did not spread through exhaled water droplets like COVID. SARS-CoV-1 had a death rate of 14 percent to 15 percent (COVID-19 is SARS-CoV-2). A SARS-CoV-1 death rate would kill 49.5 million in the United States. Vaccine mandates for COVID-19 and the resulting mass vaccinations of the public all at once could trigger a virus mutation that is vaccine resistant.

Natural Disasters. A natural disaster may hit the United States. Many predict a powerful earthquake on the West Coast. Two other threatening fault lines exist, one in the Midwest and other on the East Coast, although neither are expected to generate a crippling earthquake soon.

There is the New Madrid fault line, near the Mississippi River at the junction of Missouri, Kentucky, Illinois, Arkansas, and Tennessee. A series of strong earthquakes occurred in 1811 to 1812, so strong that they rerouted the Mississippi River. There also is the Ramapo fault line, stretching from New York to Pennsylvania and passing under 125th Street in New York City. The last earthquake generated by the fault line was in 1884.[82]

There is a giant caldera underneath Yellowstone National Park. The park sits on top of a super-volcano that is fifty-five miles long and twenty-five miles wide. Since 2015, the caldera has pushed up the ground by one inch per year, and the park also experiences many minor earthquakes each year.

There is a volcano named Cumbre Vieja, located 3,500 miles from the East Coast of the United States on the island of La Palma, part of the Canary Islands near the coast of Morocco. The volcano could explode, triggering a giant landslide that would shove part of the island into the Atlantic Ocean, generating a hundred-foot-high tsunami hurtling toward the East Coast. Evidence lies on the sea floor that such a landslide occurred once before.[83]

There was the Carrington Event, the biggest geomagnetic solar storm on record, which occurred in September 1859. A solar flare of the sun ejected a coronal mass that hit the Earth's magnetosphere. Brilliant auroras were seen around the world making the night seem like morning. Telegraph systems, "the internet of the day," over Europe and North America failed, in some cases giving telegraph operators electrical shocks, melting equipment, and causing fires.

Today a similar solar storm would cause blackouts and damage from extended electrical outages. Power surges would blow out transformers, bringing down the electrical grid. A solar storm would also knock out global positioning systems (GPS), used by cell phones and transportation systems, as well as satellites. Consider the unrest that would result should cities struggle without power for a long period of time, lacking air-conditioning, refrigeration, and public transportation. Some experts estimate the cost for the first year would be between $1 and $2 trillion and the time to recover would take four to ten years.[84] There was a solar storm in 2012, which was catastrophically strong but missed passing through Earth's orbit by a mere nine days.

Nuclear Attack. If not a solar storm, our enemies could detonate a nuclear bomb in the atmosphere above the United States, generating an electromagnetic pulse (EMP) that would knock out electrical equipment and paralyze the food supply chain, electrical service, etc. Alternatively, they could simply detonate a nuclear bomb in our major cities on the east or west coast or attack us with missles.

Second Civil War. Today, our country is as divided as it was before the Civil War. Then, it was over slavery. Today, it is over the Left's relentless drive to fundamentally transform our society into an oppression-free-woke-zone, excluding, of course, the oppression of Christians. In fact, the threat of a second Civil War is now plausible and creeping into our public discussions. A Rasmussen Reports on June 15, 2020 disclosed that one-third (34%) of voters think a second Civil War may occur in the next five years. There is no common ground between the opposing sides. The pressure cooker began to burst after the disputed 2020 election and consequent riot at the Capital on January 6, 2021.

Loss of Religious Freedom. We face an imminent loss of our religious freedom in the United States. After winning back the White House and Congress, Democrats are determined to pass the Equality Act. This legislation will require Christian churches and organizations to hire homosexuals and transgenders. Criticizing their behavior will be punished as hate speech. In 2014, the lesbian mayor of Houston, Annise Parker, subpoenaed Pastor Randy White's First Baptist Church of Katy, Texas to hand over all sermons and notes related to homosexuality and gender identity. The church refused and was successfully defended by Alliance Defending Freedom. However, is this a portent for the future?

Conclusion

Many evangelical Christian leaders believe that our country is currently under judgment from God and will face more serious judgments in the future.

The writer of Hebrews included a warning we should heed: "Marriage should be honored by all, and the marriage bed kept pure, for God will judge the adulterer and all the sexually immoral" (Hebrews 13:4).

Our country parades sin like Sodom with its Gay Pride festivities. Isaiah 3:9 states: "The look on their faces testifies against them; they parade their sin like Sodom; they do not hide it. Woe to them! They have brought disaster upon themselves."

What happened to Sodom and Gomorrah can happen to us. The apostle Peter writes: "he [God] condemned the cities of Sodom and Gomorrah by burning them to ashes, and made them an example of what is going to happen to the ungodly" (2 Peter 2:6).

We have not honored marriage in this country. We have offended God by allowing gay marriage to infect our land. We call evil good and good evil and can expect the consequences. Isaiah 5:20 states: "Woe to those who call evil good and good evil, who put darkness for light and light for darkness, who put bitter for sweet and sweet for bitter."

People who have same sex attraction or who believe they are in the wrong body are very vulnerable. The Left exploits these susceptible people by encouraging twisted sexual desires and outlawing homosexual conversion therapy. Peter writes:

> For they mouth empty, boastful words and, by appealing to the lustful desires of the flesh, they entice people who are just escaping from those who live in error. They promise them freedom, while they themselves are slaves of depravity—for "people are slaves to whatever has mastered them. (2 Peter 2:18–19)

Therefore, God has given our country over to a depraved mind. In greater numbers, people will seek out false teaching that corrupts the Bible and justifies sexual sin. Paul writes:

> For the time will come when people will not put up with sound doctrine. Instead, to suit their own desires, they will gather around them a great number of teachers to say what their itching ears want to hear. They will turn their ears away from the truth and turn aside to myths. (2 Timothy 4:3–4)

People who believe in evolution will believe in anything and are ripe for the greatest deception in history. If people believe that a single cell over time will grow to be the most complicated organism on earth through a series of random mutations, they will believe in anything. Could a Boeing 737 airplane self-assemble if given enough time? The human body is much more complicated than any airplane.

People who believe in evolution will believe that:

- Sex is harmless recreation.
- Abortion is women's health care.
- Homosexuality is normal.
- Men can marry men, and women marry women.
- Men can become women, and women become men.
- Distant national bureaucracies can best respond to local needs, and international bureaucracies can respond even better.

- The US government can indefinitely spend trillions more than it receives without consequences.
- Healthy, not sick, people must quarantine to avoid a disease that kills less than 1 percent it infects.
- An Antichrist will bring peace to the world.

6

The Urgency

The citizens of Wroclaw understand that the threat is serious, but may think the Mongols will bypass the city. Perhaps they are bogged down somewhere and will not arrive for years. What is the rush to prepare the defenses?

A leader will disclose to the people that the Mongols are taking a route that goes straight through the city. His sources tell him that the Mongols are only fifty miles away. There is no time to lose preparing the defenses.

Time is short for us as well. We have revealed the need for end times training, the cause, and the increasing peril that comes from God's judgment of America. Now, we contend that the need is urgent, and training must begin now. The signs indicate that we are very close to the rapture of the church and the tribulation.

How long do we have? We wish we could say plenty of time. However, we don't think so and will provide our reasons in this chapter.

There are many signs that we are close to the end:

- Israel has returned as a nation.
- Advanced technology makes the events described in Bible prophecy feasible.
- Many Matthew 24 signs revealed by Jesus are evident today.
- Celestial signs are manifest.
- The parable of the fig tree suggests an end date.
- Inertia for a one-world government and religion is growing.

Return of Israel

The most dramatic evidence for the end times is the return of Israel as a nation. We provided the prophecy (Isaiah 11:11–12) in chapter 1 (also see Jeremiah 16:14–15). Not only was Israel born in one day (Isaiah 66:7–8), it miraculously survived an attack the next day by six dramatically larger and better equipped Arab/Muslim countries. Israel achieved two additional miraculous victories against overwhelming odds in 1967 and 1973.

End Times Technological Capabilities

Current technology makes the end times events possible. Before the advent of television and the internet, the whole world could not simultaneously view the bodies of the two witnesses described in Revelation.

> For three and a half days some from every people, tribe, language and nation will gaze on their bodies and refuse them burial. The inhabitants of the earth will gloat over them and will celebrate by sending each other gifts, because these two prophets had tormented those who live on the earth. (Revelation 11:9–10)

Now, people don't require a television set or a computer to watch the news from around the world. All they need is their smartphones. According to Statista, as of January 2021, 55 percent of the world's global population accessed the internet with mobile devices.[85]

The end times also requires the ability to implant microchips, as suggested by the mark of the beast:

> It also forced all people, great and small, rich and poor, free and slave, to receive a mark on their right hands or on their foreheads, so that they could not buy or sell unless they had the mark, which is the name of the beast or the number of its name. (Revelation 13:16–17)

We now have implantable chips and bitcoin blockchain technology. At least three thousand Swedes have implanted chips between their thumbs and forefingers and swipe their hands to pay for merchandise and enter locked buildings.[86]

Signs in Matthew 24

In the Olivet Discourse, Jesus disclosed the signs of the end times:

> You will hear of wars and rumors of wars, but see to it that you are not alarmed. Such things must happen, but

the end is still to come. Nation will rise against nation, and kingdom against kingdom. There will be famines and earthquakes in various places. All these are the beginning of birth pains. Then you will be handed over to be persecuted and put to death, and you will be hated by all nations because of me. At that time many will turn away from the faith and will betray and hate each other, and many false prophets will appear and deceive many people. Because of the increase of wickedness, the love of most will grow cold, but the one who stands firm to the end will be saved. And this gospel of the kingdom will be preached in the whole world as a testimony to all nations, and then the end will come. (Matthew 24:6–14)

Wars and Rumors of Wars. In the twentieth century, two world wars, which increased in severity, killed more people than any time in history. On February 24, 2022 Russia invaded Ukraine, calling it a "special military operation" for the "demilitarization and denazification" of the country. This is the largest assault in Europe since World War II. Russian President Vladimir Putin had accused the democratically elected Ukrainian leaders of being "extremists" for their desire to join the European Union and NATO. To intimidate the West from joining Ukraine, Putin put his nuclear forces on high alert and warned of "consequences that you have never experienced in your history." So, here we have a war and a rumor (threat) of a nuclear war.

Famines (and Pestilences). More people died from famine during the nineteenth and twentieth centuries than any time in history. Luke 21:11 adds the word "pestilences" to famines. Revelation 6:8 lists plague, among other causes, that will kill over a fourth of the earth. COVID-19 is the second of two plagues to attack the earth in roughly the last one hundred years. The first was the Spanish flu of 1918. Both of these could foreshadow the terrible plagues to occur in Revelation 6:8.

Earthquakes. Earthquake activity has increased, as displayed in Figure 2.

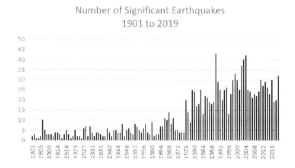

Figure 2
Source: Our World in Data[87] (change disaster category to earthquake).

Hated By All Nations. According to John Dickerson in his 2018 book *Hope of Nations*, PricewaterhouseCoopers projects that in thirty years the world's four largest economies will be 1) China, 2) India, 3) United States, 4) Indonesia.[88] He reveals that three of these countries have "muscular ideologies," such as communism in China, Hinduism in India, and Islam in Indonesia. They are not tolerant of Christianity and use force to impose their beliefs.[89]

Many Will Fall Away. The West has turned away from the Christian faith. Europe became post-Christian years ago; tourists, not worshippers, crowd their grand cathedrals. In the United States, the fastest growing demographic group is "nones," those who profess no religious affiliation.

Betray, Hate, and Lead Astray. The Left has deceived the public and made homosexuality and transgenderism seem normal, each rationalized with critical theory. The Left portrays the world as a power struggle between the oppressor and the oppressed, such as whites oppressing blacks, men oppressing women, and Christians oppressing homosexuals and transgenders. This has spawned identity politics and divided the country. The Left spews hatred with their violent riots, vulgar chants, and angry posts on social media.

Love Grow Cold. The natural desire for children is replaced by a desire for sex but without the inconvenience of raising a child, which has resulted in about 60 million abortions since 1973.

Intolerance for opposite political views is so bad in the United States that a 2021 poll by the Center for Politics at the University of Virginia found that the supporters of the two political parties would rather split into two countries than live together. "Roughly 4 in 10 (41%) of Biden and half (52%) of Trump voters at least somewhat agree that it's time to split the country, favoring blue/red states seceding from the union."[90]

Gospel Proclaimed to the World. Since the 1800s, missionaries have spread the Gospel to 58.3 percent of the unreached people groups in the world.[91] Using radio, TV, satellite, cellular, and the internet, missionary organizations can reach the remaining 42 percent within a relatively short time. The Wycliffe Bible translators plan to complete their work translating all the world languages by 2025.[92]

Missionaries now boldly penetrate the unreached frontier. For example, the Joshua Project reports that more Iranians in the past thirty years have become followers of Christ than in the past 1,000 years. The church in Africa is growing four times faster than the general population. South Korea has several churches with over one million members each. There are over seventy-five million Christians in China, and Brazil has one of the largest evangelical populations in the world.[93]

Celestial Signs

God created the sun, moon, and stars in part to serve as signs:

> And God said, "Let there be lights in the expanse of the heavens to separate the day from the night. And let them be for **signs** and for seasons, and for days and years. (Genesis 1:14) (emphasis added)

God revealed that solar and lunar eclipses would occur before the Tribulation, and by inference, the rapture. By the way, these eclipses are only possible because the sun is four hundred times wider than the moon and four hundred times farther away, making the two appear to be the same size. Isn't that an interesting "coincidence" for unbelievers?

> I will show wonders in the heavens and on the earth, blood and fire and billows of smoke. The **sun will be turned to darkness** and the **moon to blood** before the

coming of the great and dreadful day of the Lord. (Joel 2:30–31) (emphasis added)

Tetrad of Blood Moons. Pastor John Hagee and prophecy scholar Mark Blitz in their 2013 book *Four Blood Moons: Something Is About to Change* revealed that a rare tetrad (four) of blood moons would occur on four Jewish feast days during 2014 and 2015: April 15, 2014, Pesach (Passover), October 8, 2014, Sukkot (Feast of Tabernacles), April 4, 2015, Pesach, and September 28, 2015, Sukkot. This has only occurred seven times in the last 2,000 years and will not occur for another five hundred years.

When the earth is precisely aligned between the sun and the moon during a lunar eclipse, a blood moon occurs. As the moon passes through the earth's shadow, some sunlight protrudes along the edges of the earth at a low angle and makes the moon appear red, just like sunsets appear red on the horizon.

According to Hagee and Blitz, lunar eclipses are portents for Israel, signifying an imminent change, such as 1493–94, when the Jews were expelled from Spain; 1949–50, when Israel reemerged as a country after an absence of 2,000 years; and 1967–68, when Israel captured Jerusalem in the Six Days War.

However, the signs of 2014–15 may apply uniquely to the United States because all four lunar eclipses were visible in the United States, but only one was visible in Israel.

Another interesting celestial event occurred on August 21, 2017, with a total *solar* eclipse that crossed the entire contiguous United States and was visible only in the United States. A solar eclipse occurs when the moon is precisely aligned between the sun and the earth, blocking the sun as viewed from earth. The last time a total solar eclipse crossed the length of the United States was one hundred years ago on June 8, 1918.

The 2017 eclipse entered the United States in Oregon and exited in South Carolina. When it reached Oregon, the sun was setting in Jerusalem. Oddly, the eclipse's path crossed Salem, Oregon; Salem, Idaho; Salem, Wyoming; Salem, Nebraska; Salem, Missouri; Salem,

Kentucky; and Salem, South Carolina; a total of seven Salems. Salem is short for Jerusalem.

The next total solar eclipse to cross the entire United States will occur in 2024, entering in Texas and exiting in Maine. The paths of the 2017 and 2024 eclipses form an X in Southern Illinois, near the New Madrid fault.

Parable of the Fig Tree

Numerous verses, such as Hosea 9:10, refer to Israel as a fig tree.

> When I found Israel, it was like finding grapes in the desert; when I saw your ancestors, it was like seeing the early fruit on the fig tree. (Hosea 9:10a)

Jesus told the parable of the fig tree in Matthew 24:32–34, which is a dramatic sign that we are near the end of the age:

> Now learn this lesson from the fig tree: As soon as its twigs get tender and its leaves come out, you know that summer is near. Even so, when you see all these things, you know that it [end times] is near, right at the door. Truly I tell you, this generation will certainly not pass away until all these things have happened.

Tender twigs and leaves coming out could indicate that the fig was recently planted. Israel was recently "planted" in 1948.

The span of a generation is seventy or eighty years:

> Our days may come to seventy years, or eighty, if our strength endures. (Psalm 90:10a)

Therefore, Jesus's second coming would occur in 2028 (1948 + 80 = 2028), and the rapture in 2021 (2028 − 7 = 2021), but this specific timing did not work out. We must remember what Jesus said about predictions such as this, "But about that day or hour no one knows, not even the angels in heaven, nor the Son, but only the Father" (Matthew 24:36).

One-World Government and Religion

One World Government. Revelation 13 reveals the prophecy of a one-world government, in which the Antichrist rules over every nation:

> It [Antichrist] was given power to wage war against God's holy people and to conquer them. And it was given authority over every tribe, people, language and nation. (Revelation 13:7)

The West has longed for a one-world government for one hundred years, since the League of Nations was founded on January 10, 1920. At that time, forty-two member nations joined but not the United States. The League was dissolved in 1946 and replaced by the United Nations. Four times more nations (193 nations) joined, including the United States.

Today, the World Economic Forum (WEF) promotes the "Great Reset," in which "the world must act jointly and swiftly to revamp all aspects of our societies and economies ... Every country ... and every industry ... must be transformed. In short, we need a 'Great Reset' of capitalism."[94] The forum attracts the world's top political, business, and social leaders. The founder and executive chairman of the WEF, Klaus Schwab said, "the pandemic [COVID-19] represents a rare but narrow window of opportunity to reflect, reimagine, and reset our world to create a healthier, more equitable, and more prosperous future."[94]

How? By imposing coordinated wealth taxes throughout the world, large-scale green spending programs, and wealth redistribution. In short, they are advocating global socialism and intend to replace corporate stockholders with left-wing bureaucrats and climate change zealots. In November 2016 the WEF tweeted that in the year 2030, "You'll own nothing, and you'll be happy."[95]

One-World Religion. Revelation 17 reveals the prophecy of a one-world religion, described as "the great prostitute":

One of the seven angels who had the seven bowls came
and said to me, "Come, I will show you the punishment
of the great prostitute, who sits by many waters.
(Revelation 17:1)

According to noted prophecy scholar Dr. John F. Walvoord, "The
great prostitute described in these verses [Revelation 17:1–6] is a
portrayal of apostate Christendom in the end time," after true believers
have left via the rapture.[96]

The religion is worldwide:

Then the angel said to me, "The waters you saw, where
the prostitute sits, are peoples, multitudes, nations and
languages. (Revelation 17:15)

The one-world religion works closely with the world political
powers:

With her the kings of the earth committed adultery,
and the inhabitants of the earth were intoxicated with
the wine of her adulteries. (Revelation 17:2)

According to Walvoord, "the apostasy, called adultery and
fornication here, of course refers to spiritual unfaithfulness, not to
physical adultery."[96] However, might the religion tolerate and even
celebrate sexual sin? Perhaps the leaders of the earth will align with this
progressive religion, and the citizens of the earth will practice sexual sin
with wild abandon as if drunk.

The world religion will eventually persecute and kill Christians:

I saw that the woman was drunk with the blood of God's
holy people, the blood of those who bore testimony to
Jesus. (Revelation 17:6)

Conclusion

The second coming and the rapture, which precedes the second coming, are drawing near. Although no one can predict when this will occur, the warning signs are accumulating like the water rising behind a dam. The time to train is now.

However, training always faces headwinds. There are obstacles to overcome. Christians in the United States face significant opposition, which is discussed next.

7

The Opposition

I t won't be long before a faction in Wroclaw will suggest that a national army may come to save them. Why not just wait? If no army appears, then appease the Golden Horde: surrender, pay tribute to the Mongols, and live as best they can under Mongol rule. After all, life under subjugation is better than no life at all.

A leader could stiffen the resolve to defend the city. He will explain that a national army has already been defeated in battle, and Wroclaw is left to defend itself. No, he will argue, life under *subjugation* is no life at all. They will lose their culture, history, and way of life. They will lose their independence and become slaves to a foreign master, not to the God of their fathers. Surrender is not an option, and they must see to their own defense.

We too must stiffen our resolve. So far, we have discussed the need to train for the end times prompted by the disappearance of the Christian worldview in America. We have provided the evidence that God, our coach, is real; His holy word, the Bible, is true; and the Bible predicts the future. We have reviewed the prophetic sequence of events that the Bible predicts. We have explained how sexual sin has led to God's judgment and disclosed the signs that indicate that the end is near. Now, we will reveal the forces that oppose us.

There are always headwinds to overcome when training. Ours is a growing totalitarian state opposed to biblically-based Christian free speech, and one that is progressively resembling the totalitarian state in Communist China. This growing totalitarianism in the United States began at the close of the Sexual Revolution.

Consequence of the Sexual Revolution

Author Rod Dreher pronounced that evangelical Christians lost the sexual revolution battle. As he wrote in the *Benedict Option*, April 2015 was the beginning of the end:

> The steady decline of Christianity and the steady increase in hostility to traditional values came to a head in April 2015, when the state of Indiana passed a version of the federal Religious Freedom Restoration Act. The law merely provided a valid religious liberty defense for those sued for discrimination. It did not guarantee that those

> defendants would prevail. Gay rights activist loudly protested, calling the law bigoted—and for the first time ever, big business took sides in the culture war, coming down firmly on behalf of gay rights. Indiana backed down under corporate pressure—as did Arkansas a week later.
>
> This was a watershed event. It showed that if big business objected, even Republican politicians in red states would not take a stand, even a mild one, for religious freedom. Professing orthodox biblical Christianity on sexual matters was now thought to be evidence of intolerable bigotry. Conservative Christians had been routed. We were living in a new country.[97]

Since then, the Republican National Committee has announced a "Pride Coalition" with a LGBT advocacy group called the "Log Cabin Republicans."

The sexual revolution has spawned a movement like the Chinese cultural revolution. Initiated by Mao Zedong and led by youthful radicals, the cultural revolution, from 1966 to 1976, attempted to purge capitalists and traditional elements from Chinese society after the failure of Mao's Great Leap Forward program (1958–1962). Students denounced teachers, and children denounced parents. Those who let slip a counterrevolutionary thought were sent to reeducation camps.

Parallel of Chinese and US Cultural Revolutions

Here are some specific parallels between the cultural revolution in China and the present cultural revolution we are experiencing in the United States.

Objective

Chinese: Purge bourgeois elements from society.
United States: Purge "white supremacy, homophobia, transphobia" from society.

Organizing Theory

Chinese: Mao Zedong Thought
United States: Critical Theory

Shock Troops

Chinese: Red Guard (student led)
United States: Antifa, Black Lives Matter, college students

Destruction of Historical Relics

Chinese: Red Guards destroyed churches, temples, mosques, monasteries, Temple of Heaven, Ming Tombs, Temple of Confucius.
United States: Protestors deface or pull-down Christopher Columbus statues in Boston, Miami, Pittsburgh, and St. Paul. Confederate symbols in the South are removed.

Police Intervention Suspended

Chinese: Chinese Communist Party (CCP) lifted restraints on Red Guard violent behavior, and the National Police Chief pardoned Red Guards.
United States: Police refuse to interfere with "mostly peaceful protests," which were actual riots during 2020 that caused $2 billion of damage and killed scores of people. George Soros-backed district attorneys in Philadelphia, St. Louis, San Francisco, and other cities have stopped prosecuting crimes such as disorderly conduct, vagrancy, and loitering. The San Francisco DA will not prosecute "victimless" crimes and "small" thefts.

Replace Local Governments

Chinese: Revolutionary committees replaced local government.
United States: Revolutionary CHAZ autonomous zone in Seattle replaces local government in the Capitol Hill neighborhood.

Forced reeducation

Chinese: Those deemed reactionary and counterrevolutionary are forced to the "down to the countryside" reeducation camps.

United States: Required critical race theory indoctrination classes are mandated in schools and corporations. For example, the Heritage Foundation reports that Sandia National Nuclear Laboratories conducted a reeducation camp for white male executives to expose their hidden white supremacist attitudes and to require apology letters from them.[98]

Sloganeering

Chinese: Call opponents counterrevolutionaries, bourgeois, running dogs, and revisionists.

United States: Call opponents haters, homophobes, transphobes, white supremacists, and racists.

Public Shaming

Chinese: "Struggle Sessions" forced victims to admit imagined crimes after verbal and physical abuse by crowds and ritual humiliation by wearing dunce caps. The objective was to eliminate counterrevolutionary deviationism thinking and shape public opinion to correspond to CCP dogmas.

United States: Social justice warriors on Twitter force victims to apologize or be fired for deviationism from Leftist orthodoxy. For example, former NBA Sacramento Kings announcer Grant Napear was forced to resign after tweeting "all lives matter."

Creeping Totalitarianism Resembling China

According to Dreher, a soft totalitarianism is emerging in the United States, imposing a new ideology but without the gulags of the Soviet Union. A totalitarian regime controls what a society says and thinks, upends traditions and institutions, and imposes a new ideology. Rulers define what is true and force everyone to agree. In the words of the

Italian fascist Benito Mussolini, totalitarianism is "all within the state, none outside the state, none against the state."[99]

Our country is beginning to resemble the Chinese totalitarian state with censorship of ideas, promotion of abortion, revision of history, redefinition of language, and behavior modification.

Censorship of Ideas

China: The CCP blocks Google, YouTube, Facebook, and Twitter in China.

United States: If you disagree with leftist ideology or fail to use leftist language, you are censored. Here is how it is done. The leftist Southern Poverty Law Center (SPLC), first provides the leftist elites with cover and justification for censorship. The SPLC brands mainstream Christian organizations like Focus on the Family, Alliance Defending Freedom, and American Family Association as "hate groups," so the media, education, corporations, and government can censor them.

Then, businesses exclude Christian organizations from programs and censor their products. For example, Amazon denies Christian organizations labeled as "hate groups" by the SPLC from participating in Amazon's charity arm, Amazon Smile. Amazon also bans books critical of transgenderism, such as *When Harry Became Sally,* produced by the Heritage Foundation, a mainstream conservative think tank. Twitter routinely suspends Christian organizations, like Focus on the Family, for "misgendering" transsexuals (referencing them by their biological sex). Twitter also permanently banned the President of the United States Donald Trump and banned for a time the oldest newspaper in the United States, the *New York Post.*

Promotion of Abortion

China: The state once outlawed families from producing more than one child, forced abortions, and caused an imbalance of 30 million more men than women because families chose to keep male babies and abort female babies.

United States: The federal government gives more than $500 million to Planned Parenthood each year. The state of New York passed a law allowing abortion up to the moment of delivery.

Revision of History

China: The state has erased all evidence of the 1989 Tiananmen Square Massacre.

United States: The *New York Times* promotes the Pulitzer Prize winning "1619 Project," and thousands of primary and secondary schools in the United States use it. This leftist propaganda claims the United States was founded in 1619, the year twenty "slaves" arrived, and the Revolutionary War was fought primarily to preserve slavery. This, of course, is patently false. First, Virginia was an English Colony in 1619; the United States was founded 168 years later. Second, in 1619 slavery was outlawed in Virginia; slave codes weren't instituted until 1705. Third, the so-called slaves were indentured servants, like many in the white labor force, who were freed in five to seven years. But since the 1619 Project is promoted by the *New York Times*, it is accepted as fact.

Redefinition of Language

China: The CCP is building a surveillance state similar to that portrayed in George Orwell's book *1984*. To enforce censorship, the government employs thousands of individuals to monitor personal letters, telephone calls, social media postings and online news and advertising. Forbidden terms include "Dalai Lama" (symbol of Tibetan independence), "Tibet independence," "Go, Hong Kong" (support for Hong Kong prodemocracy protests), "great firewall of China" (Chinese censorship), "dictatorship" (suggestion that China is a dictatorship), "Tiananmen" (1989 prodemocracy protests), etc.

The government undermines information it finds objectionable. After the Chinese takeover of Hong Kong, the CCP accused protestors of being "rumor mongers" who "subvert state power" and oppose "One China."

United States: The Left redefines language to frame its arguments and put the opposition on the defensive. For example, the 2021 U.S.

House of Representatives introduced new house rules that would ban "father, mother, son, daughter, etc." in legislation as too biased and insufficiently inclusive.

In fact, the Left has created a long list of code words and euphemisms, which are repeated by all the leftist elites in government, media, education, and the corporate world. One such word is "inclusivity." Who can be against inclusivity? However, used by the Left it means compulsory acceptance of LGBTQ ideology that gender is what you choose, and homosexual behavior is normal. "Inequity" is another term used by the Left. Again, who can be against inequity? However, used by the Left it means compulsory acceptance of critical theory that all minorities are victims of oppression.

There are many other code words and euphemisms:

- "Social justice" is a euphemism for promoting leftist causes.
- "Reproductive health care, women's right to choose, and pro-choice" are euphemisms for killing a child in the womb.
- "Rights" is a sleight-of-hand to alter societal norms. For example, "gay rights" implies that gays are denied certain rights, but the fact is that gays have the exact same rights as nongays: gays can marry someone of the opposite sex just like nongays. "Gay rights" in fact changes the *meaning* of marriage and *forces* everyone to say that what homosexuals do is marriage.

Modification of Behavior

China: The Chinese are rolling out a national social credit system that monitors the behavior of individuals, corporations, and government organizations, rewarding those with a high social credit scores and punishing those with low scores. For now, corporations, local government, and the national government operate different systems, some on a voluntary basis, but in the future the national government will absorb those systems and monitor everybody. Low scores are given for bad driving, jaywalking, smoking in nonsmoking zones, buying and playing too many video games, posting fake or forbidden news on social media, making frivolous purchases, not paying fines or bills on time, and playing music too loud on trains. Punishments include lower internet speeds; banishment from flights, trains, and better hotels; exclusion from the best schools and jobs; and difficulty getting dates online, obtaining bank loans, and making purchases. Rewards include sped-up applications for loans, etc., waiver of down payments, purchase discounts, and lower interest rates.

United States: Although the US government is not building a social credit system per se like China, corporations are introducing elements of a soft social credit system. For example, PayPal now teams with the Southern Poverty Law Center to share information with financial firms and politicians about those they deem "white supremacist" and "antigovernment" instigators. Likewise, Facebook and Microsoft are identifying and monitoring "extremists." Some banks have banned firearms purchases, which are perfectly legal transactions.

The Left in the United States Equals the CCP in China

China is a one-party state. Twenty-five top officials of the CCP control a population of 1.4 billion. The United States is not a one-party state but functions as one. The Left in the United States controls the major power sources, such as big education, big tech, big corporations, and big government. Together they exert control like the CCP does in China.

Big Education. Public primary and secondary schools are essentially government schools ruled by an elected school board. Most big city school boards are controlled by people who support leftist ideology. There are private and home school options, but most citizens can't afford them. Attendance at school is compulsory and failure to comply can result in truancy fines, imprisonment, and possible loss of child custody. The vast majority of parents have no other option than to send their children to government schools.

Big Education is dominated by federal and state departments of education and colleges of education that train teachers. Both are thoroughly infiltrated by LGBTQ ideology. This trickles down to local communities. For example, according to a *World* magazine, beginning in September 2020 "New Jersey public schools will teach children in grades five, six, eight, 10 and 12 about the great historical contributions of LGBTQ people to the United States history."[100] Illinois has passed a law requiring that government schools teach LGBTQ history to students by the eighth grade.

Comprehensive Sexuality Education has also infiltrated government schools. Sponsored by SIECUS (the Sexuality Information Education Council), Planned Parenthood, teachers' unions, and the ACLU, Comprehensive Sexuality Education claims to protect children from bullying and prevent unwanted pregnancies and sexually transmitted diseases. In fact, it normalizes sex outside of marriage, homosexual behavior, and transgenderism. For example, beginning in kindergarten, teachers explain that sex assigned at birth may not match the child's "true" gender identity. Middle school students are taught about oral and anal sex. High schoolers are shown how to use condoms, urged to explore their gender identities and sexual orientations, and reassured that homosexuality is quite normal. Children of any age are briefed about their rights to receive birth control and abortion services without their parents' knowledge.

The Madison School District in Wisconsin allowed children to transition to a different gender and use a different name at school without notifying the parents or obtaining their consent. The California Teachers Association also advocates a similar policy.

Big Tech. Author Douglas Murray in the *Madness of Crowds: Gender, Race, and Identity*, reports that Google search is blatantly biased. It deliberately floods search results with material that agrees with the leftist causes it supports, such as gay marriage.[101]

Murray conducted an experiment searching for images of gay couples and straight couples. When he searched for "gay couple," he got what he was searching for: image after image of handsome, happy gay couples. However, when he searched for "straight couple,"

> at least one to two images in each of the five images was of a lesbian couple or a couple of gay men. Within just a couple of rows of images for "straight couple' there are actually more photographs of gay couples then there are of straight ones.[102]

When searching for "straight white couple," Murray reports that one of the first images was a close-up photo of a knuckle with "HATE" written on it. The third image was of a black couple. In contrast, when searching for "Asian couple," there were image after image of male and female Asian pairs, with zero gay couples. In an era with very sophisticated facial recognition technology, something is clearly amiss. Google is trying to mold public opinion to conform to leftist ideology.

Parler is a libertarian alternative to Facebook and Twitter and once the #1 download app in the Apple Store. However, Apple and Google removed the app from their online stores, and later Amazon Web Services (AWS) shut down Parler after the January 6, 2001, US capital break-in. Why? AWS claimed that "they [Parler] were unable to effectively identify and remove content that encourages or incites violence."[103]

However, addressing the AWS action, author and former *New York Times* reporter Alex Berenson retorted, "All the stuff on Parler you can find on Twitter and Facebook."[103] This was confirmed later after a Department of Justice investigation determined that the primary social media platform used by the January 6 instigators was Facebook, not Parler.[104]

Dennis Prager is a popular conservative radio talk-show host, writer, and founder of PragerU, which provides short videos addressing issues from a conservative perspective. YouTube has placed many of the videos on the "restricted list," making them inaccessible to schools and libraries, slapped warnings that indicate objectionable content on the videos, and added editorial comments redirecting viewers to sites offering contradictory views. Which videos have content so objectionable that the public must be warned, shielded, and redirected? Videos addressing the Ten Commandments, Winston Churchill, and the causes of the Korean War.[105]

Big Corporations. Most big corporations today support LGBTQ causes, including the foundations for Wells Fargo, Levi Strauss, GE, Walmart, Macys, and Verizon.[106] According to the Human Rights Campaign, nearly half (233) of the Fortune 500 achieved a perfect score of 100 on the HRC "Equality" Index.[107]

Big corporations proudly display their support of the sexual revolution. Whole Foods sponsors Drag Queen Story Hours. *TeenVogue*, a magazine targeting preteen and teenaged girls, broadcasts "Having Sex when You're Fat: Tips on Positions, Props and Preparations,"[108] and publishes an op-ed that explains that "Sex Work Is Real Work."[109]

The National Basketball Association was confident enough to pull their all-star game out of Charlotte, North Carolina, because the state passed a bill that would prevent biological males from using female public restrooms. The National Football League threatened to prevent Texas from hosting future Super Bowls if the state passed a bill similar to North Carolina's.

Big Government. Ultimately, big government is most formidable because it possesses the power of the sword and reaches everywhere with its many agencies and quasi-public organizations. Public Broadcasting's Sesame Street features a drag queen activist, Billy Porter. Public libraries feature Drag Queen Story Hour. State human rights commissions force small businesses to comply with leftist ideology.

For example, Blaine Adamson, owner of Hands-on Originals, a Christian-owned shop in Lexington, Kentucky, which creates customized T-shirts, caps, etc., was asked by a gay organization to print T-shirts for a local gay pride festival. Adamson refused because of his Christian faith and referred the organization to another shop. The organization filed a complaint with the Lexington-Fayette Urban County Human Rights Commission, who ruled against Adamson, ordering him to print whatever the gay organization wanted and to undergo diversity training. This is tantamount to forcing a Jewish printer to create a T-shirt for a neo-Nazi organization. Seven years later at the Kentucky Supreme Court, Adamson prevailed when the court ruled that the government cannot compel expression.

During the COVID-19 panic, governments arbitrarily closed churches or grossly limited their attendance while exempting certain commercial organizations. In Chicago, Mayor Lori Lightfoot threatened to tear down the Elim Romanian Pentecostal Church building if more than ten people met in its 1,300-seat sanctuary after the church repeatedly refused to comply with the city's orders.[110] The U.S. government has issued mandates that force U.S. government and military personnel, large corporations, and healthcare workers to get vaccinated, be tested weekly, or else lose their jobs. This forces people to be inoculated with an experimental gene therapy that mitigates disease symptoms but does not prevent disease infection or transmission.

On September 9, 2021 President Joe Biden warned, "We've been patient, but our patience is wearing thin. Your refusal has cost us all," implying that the unvaccinated were the ones causing the widespread deaths. Whereupon, he mandated that federal government employees and contractors, affecting 2.1 million people, be vaccinated with no option to opt out and be tested. Comply or lose your job! In addition, he mandated that the following be vaccinated or produce a negative Covid test at least once a week:

- Employers with 100 or more employees, affecting two-thirds of the country's workforce, about 100 million people.
- Health care facilities that receive Medicare or Medicaid, affecting 7 million workers at 50,000 health care providers.

What is disturbing is that these mandates are widely *accepted*, not challenged, by the public. A January 2022 Rasmussen Report, "COVID-19: Democratic Voters Support Harsh Measures Against Unvaccinated," disclosed the authoritarian lengths that many Democrats will go to punish the unvaccinated:

- 59% support the government requiring home-confinement for the unvaccinated.
- 48% support the government fining or imprisoning those who publicly question the effectiveness of the COVID-19 vaccine.
- 45% support temporary imprisonment in quarantine camps of those who refuse the vaccine.
- 29% support the government temporarily removing custody of children from parents who refuse the vaccine.

Recently, the Religions Exemption Accountability Project (REAP), on behalf of LGBTQ students, filed a class-action lawsuit against the Department of Education. REAP claims the department allows religious schools that receive federal funds to "discriminate" against

LGBTQ students. REAP brands Christian schools, such as Liberty University, as homophobic for faithfully adhering to their Christian convictions, which were known to students before they enrolled.

Churches will be targeted next if the "Equality" Act is passed. The Act's name is leftist-speak at its worst. In reality, it should be called the Religious Persecution Act because it would add sexual orientation and gender identity to the 1964 Civil Rights Act. If passed, it would force churches to hire homosexuals or transgenders, allow them to participate in children's programs, and allow transgender women (biological males) to use women's bathrooms.

Conclusion

The growing totalitarianism in the United States opposes Christianity and will eventually curtail Christian freedoms. Closely resembling China, it will accelerate the trend to form a one-world government. We must develop the spiritual disciplines now to survive in such a challenging environment. That is the subject of the next chapter.

8

The Plan

In Wroclaw the remnant who refuses to surrender must shoulder the burden to defend the city. The leader must explain what to do and assign tasks. They must strengthen the weak points on the citadel ramparts. They must gather and store food and water, repair their weapons and drill, and steel their courage and resolve. There is no time to lose. Each person has a job to do and a skill to employ.

We too, must prepare. Now is not the time to sit in shock as God judges the United States or wallow in despondency as we are reduced to a second-rate power. We must not be agitated by the news or retreat to a bunker and wait for the end. As the apostle Paul asks in Romans 8:35: "Who shall separate us from the love of Christ? Shall trouble or hardship or persecution or famine or nakedness or danger or sword?" He answers in verse 37: "No, in all these things we are more than conquerors through him who loved us."

When all is crumbling around us, how then can we be conquerors? That is what we will discuss in this chapter. In fact, our finest hour draws near!

Our mission? To stand firm at our post, fight the good fight, save the remnant, and wait for Jesus to relieve us. This is a unique opportunity, the most exciting time in human history, and we get to play a part.

Just think, God chose us for this time before the creation of the world!

> For he chose us in him before the creation of the world to be holy and blameless in his sight. In love he predestined us for adoption to sonship through Jesus Christ, in accordance with his pleasure and will. (Ephesians 1:4–5)

Our priorities are to live holy lives, spread the Gospel, and wait expectantly for Jesus's return. Now, more than ever, we need to provide salt and light to a dying world. If we live victoriously, people will notice, and many will enter into God's kingdom.

We expect some tough times for followers of Jesus between now and the Rapture as listed in Table 1. Future Tough Times.

Expected Challenges for Christians before the Rapture	
Category	Challenge
Economy	Inflation and deficits accelerate. Unemployment grows.
Staples	Prices for food/water increase. Two-to-three-week disruption of grocery store supply chains occur due to natural disasters, cyberattacks, or pandemics.
Free Speech	Big Tech continues to censor anti-LGBTQ language, and companies fire employees over anti-LGBTQ language.
Government	The Equality Act is passed. Blue state Christian companies and churches must hire LGBTQ employees. Some pastors are imprisoned, and some churches are closed. Riots continue in blue state cities every time a black person is killed by police. Urban centers become less safe with police defunding and retirements. Violence increases with gangs fighting over turf.
Environment	Hurricanes, tornadoes, earthquakes, and ongoing pandemics occur.

Table 1. Future Tough Times

This chapter prepares us for hardship and persecution. We must plan, prepare, and persevere. We discuss planning and preparation in this chapter and perseverance in the next chapter. It is possible to live joyfully amidst the turmoil.

Planning

Planning prevents anxiety. The first step is to confront your worries. Then, plan for what you can control and surrender what you cannot to God.

The Bible endorses planning.

> Go to the ant, you sluggard; consider its ways and be
> wise! It has no commander, no overseer or ruler, yet it

stores its provisions in summer and gathers its food at harvest. (Proverbs 6:6–8)

Suppose one of you wants to build a tower. Won't you first sit down and estimate the cost to see if you have enough money to complete it? (Luke 14:28)

SMART Goals. In this chapter, we will use the popular SMART goals acronym to plan:

- Specific: clear and unambiguous
- Measurable: can measure your progress
- Achievable: attainable and not impossible
- Realistic: within reach within the time specified
- Timely: includes a starting date and a target date

Spiritual Warfare

The Democrat party, courts, education, entertainment, sports, Big Tech, and Big Business have teamed up to promote the LGBTQ ideology. However, it is not some vast human conspiracy. It is too widespread and ingenious for humans to devise. Rather, it is evidence of spiritual warfare. It has the imprint of Satan, the enemy.

Our country's original sin was slavery, for which God judged us with the Civil War. Now, the enemy is throwing that sin back in our face by inventing an ingenious ideology called critical theory, a variation of Marxism. Karl Marx attempted to pit the working class against capitalists. Today, leftists pit blacks/Hispanics against whites, women against men, homosexuals against heterosexuals, and transgenders against biological sexes. Critical theory camouflages sexual sin by expressing it as a right, such as reproductive health care rights, gay rights, and transgender rights.

This is spectacularly devious, an act of evil genius. Reproductive health care "rights" actually permit killing another human being. Gay "rights" actually redefine marriage; transgender "rights" actually redefine maleness and femaleness; and both force compliance by all.

Therefore, our end-times enemy is found in the spiritual realm.

> Finally, be strong in the Lord and in his mighty power. Put on the full armor of God, so that you can take your stand against the devil's schemes. For our struggle is not against flesh and blood, but against the rulers, against the authorities, against the powers of this dark world and against the **spiritual forces of evil in the heavenly realms**. Therefore put on the full armor of God, so that when the day of evil comes, you may be able to stand your ground, and after you have done everything, to stand. (Ephesians 6:10–13) (emphasis added)

We battle not against people but against the spiritual realm. Our enemy is Satan and his demons. Satan has misled people and recruited them into his cause. Christians who understand biblical doctrine can discern this and avoid the "cunning and craftiness of people in their deceitful scheming. Instead, speaking the truth in love, we will grow to become in every respect the mature body of him who is the head, that is, Christ." (Ephesians 4:14b–15)

Spiritual Weapons

To battle a spiritual enemy, we require spiritual weapons:

> Therefore put on the full armor of God, so that when the day of evil comes, you may be able to stand your ground, and after you have done everything, to stand. Stand firm then, with the **belt of truth** buckled around your waist, with the **breastplate of righteousness** in place, and with your **feet fitted with the readiness that comes from the gospel of peace**. In addition to all this, take up the **shield of faith**, with which you can extinguish all the flaming arrows of the evil one. Take the **helmet of salvation** and the **sword of the Spirit**, which is the word of God. And pray in the Spirit on all occasions with all kinds of prayers and requests. (Ephesians 6:13–18a) (emphasis added)

We will discuss each of these weapons, including their use, the associated spiritual disciplines to follow, the applicable spiritual gifts to employ, and the crowns to win in heaven. Please see Table 2. Spiritual Weapons Arsenal. Spiritual gifts and crowns are thoroughly discussed in our book *Training Guide for Heaven: Running for the Prize*. The Bible describes spiritual gifts, or special abilities meant to serve the church, in verses such as Romans 12:6–8. The Holy Spirit conveys spiritual gifts when a person accepts Jesus Christ as Savior. Crowns are rewards for the believer in heaven for victorious living on earth, and crowns may also convey positions of responsibility in heaven.

An Arsenal of Spiritual Weapons					
Weapons		Employment		Specialist	Reward
Roman Soldier	Christian	Use	Spiritual Discipline	Spiritual Gift	Crown
Belt	Truth	Be alert and discerning; live not by lies	• Bible study • Prayer	• Prophecy • Wisdom • Knowledge	Crown of Glory
Breastplate	Righteousness	Be steadfast; stand firm against sexual sin	• Holy Living	• Encouragement	Crown of Righteousness
Sandals (feet)	Readiness	Be prepared to share faith through service	• Service • Giving • Evangelism	• Service • Mercy • Giving • Evangelism	Soul Winner's Crown
Shield	Faith	Be strong; gird yourself for ambush	• Confession • Fellowship • Worship • Bible study • Prayer • Fasting	• Faith • Leadership	Crown of Life
Helmet	Salvation	Be courageous and bold	• Evangelism	• Evangelism	Soul Winner's Crown
Sword	Word of God	Be wise; know Bible doctrine	• Bible study	• Teaching • Wisdom	Victor's Crown

Table 2. Spiritual Weapons Arsenal

Anyone can use the spiritual weapons discussed here. It is not necessary to possess the spiritual gift. All of us must employ these spiritual weapons during the end times. Those who possess spiritual gifts are weapons specialists, superusers with special spiritual power.

Belt of Truth

Roman Soldier's Weapon: A Roman soldier wore a six to eight-inch belt (balteus) on which he would hang his body armor and weapons.

Christian's Weapon: Our belt is absolute truth. On this hang all the other spiritual weapons.

Use: In our post-Christian nation, truth has become relative, something subject to each individual's taste. In a totalitarianism state, the elites define truth. They use the power of propaganda and deception to indoctrinate the population with their ideology. They force compliance. Our weapon is knowledge of absolute truth. Its source? Jesus.

> You are a king, then!" said Pilate. Jesus answered, "You say that I am a king. In fact, **the reason I was born and came into the world is to testify to the truth**. Everyone on the side of truth listens to me." (John 18:37) (emphasis added)

Jesus came to earth to "testify to the truth." If you want to know the truth, you must listen to Jesus. It is important that we know the truth and speak it plainly.

> Rather, we have renounced secret and shameful ways; we do not use deception, nor do we distort the word of God. On the contrary, by setting forth the truth plainly we commend ourselves to everyone's conscience in the sight of God. (2 Corinthians 4:2)

As Christian Soviet dissident Alexander Solzhenitsyn said, we must "live not by lies." For example, as reported by Rod Dreher in his book *Live Not by Lies: A Manual for Christian Dissent*, Solzhenitsyn committed to the following:

- Will not say, write, affirm, or distribute anything that distorts the truth
- Will not go to a demonstration or participate in a collective action unless fully supportive of the cause
- Will not take part in a meeting in which the discussion is forced and no one can speak the truth
- Will not vote for a candidate or proposal that is dubious or unworthy
- Will walk out of an event as soon as the speaker utters a lie, ideological drivel, or shameless propaganda
- Will not support journalism that distorts or hides the underlying facts[111]

Of course, truth telling carries the risk of censure:

Truth is nowhere to be found, and whoever shuns evil becomes a prey. (Isaiah 59:15b)

Lies lurk everywhere, and we must be alert and discerning. For example, our country is stained with the blood of abortion and falsely calls it reproductive health care.

For your hands are stained with blood, your fingers with guilt. Your lips have spoken falsely, and your tongue mutters wicked things. (Isaiah 59:3)

Our country is deeply divided over the lies of systematic racism, gay marriage, and transgenderism. The Left has incited "rebellion and treachery against the Lord, turning our backs on our God, inciting revolt and oppression, uttering lies our hearts have conceived" (Isaiah 59:13).

Spiritual Discipline: We wield our weapon, the belt of truth, by studying the Bible, praying, and asking the Holy Spirit for insight.

As Christians we must discern the truth from lies and never affirm the lies. When we hear "gay marriage," we respond with biblical marriage:

> That is why a man leaves his father and mother and is united to his wife, and they become one flesh. (Genesis 2:24)

When we hear "women's reproductive health care," we respond with biblical conception:

> Your eyes saw my unformed body; all the days ordained for me were written in your book before one of them came to be. (Psalm 139:16)

When we hear "evolution" we respond with biblical creation:

> In the beginning God created the heavens and the earth. (Genesis 1:1)

When we hear "transgender," we respond with biblical gender:

> He created them male and female and blessed them. And he named them "Mankind" when they were created. (Genesis 5:2)

When we hear "racism," we respond with biblical mankind (one race):

> This is the written account of Adam's family line. When God created mankind, he made them in the likeness of God. (Genesis 5:1)

Spiritual Gift: People who possess the spiritual gift of prophecy are specially equipped to discern truth from lies and proclaim biblical truth. In addition, people who have the spiritual gift of wisdom and knowledge are specially equipped to spot the lies hidden in propaganda and euphemistic language.

Crown: The crown of glory (1 Peter 5:2–4) will be given to those Christian leaders who humbly shepherd their flock, in part by proclaiming the truth of the Bible.

SMART Goal Example: To remain anchored in the truth, in three months I will memorize the five Bible verses listed above and will recite them audibly or mentally every time I hear or read the lie expressed.

Breastplate of Righteousness

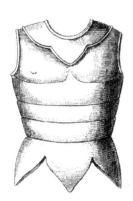

Roman Soldier's Weapon: A Roman soldier wore a breastplate (cuirass) made of bronze to protect his vital organs.

Christian's Weapon: Our breastplate is righteousness, by standing firm against sin, especially sexual sin. Righteousness provides the authority to proclaim what is morally right. We must therefore function as judges. However, we cannot judge if we are blinded by our own sin.

Many people falsely conclude that Matthew 7:1–3 forbids judging other peoples' practices:

> Do not judge, or you too will be judged. For in the same way you judge others, you will be judged, and with the measure you use, it will be measured to you. Why do you look at the speck of sawdust in your brother's eye and pay no attention to the plank in your own eye? (Matthew 7:1–3)

They ignore verse 5 that says to remove the plank in your own eye before you judge another person. In other words, don't be a hypocrite:

> You hypocrite, first take the plank out of your own eye, and then you will see clearly to remove the speck from your brother's eye. (Matthew 7:5)

They also ignore verse 6, which clearly instructs us to judge another person's suitability to hear biblical truth:

> Do not give dogs what is sacred; do not throw your pearls to pigs. If you do, they may trample them under their feet, and turn and tear you to pieces. (Matthew 7:6)

Use: As Christians we must not bow to the immense social pressure to normalize sexual sin, including adultery, fornication, pornography, homosexuality, transgenderism, abortion, and divorce. We must take a firm stand against this unrighteousness.

> Do not conform to the pattern of this world, but be transformed by the renewing of your mind. Then you will be able to test and approve what God's will is—his good, pleasing and perfect will. (Romans 12:2)

God is with us when we take a firm stand for righteousness:

> The Lord detests the way of the wicked, but he loves those who pursue righteousness. (Proverbs 15:9)

> The eyes of the Lord are on the righteous, and his ears are attentive to their cry; but the face of the Lord is against those who do evil, to blot out their name from the earth. (Psalm 34:15-16)

God will reward us for standing firm for righteousness:

> Blessed are those who are persecuted because of righteousness, for theirs is the kingdom of heaven. (Matthew 5:10)

We live in a constitutional republic with explicit free speech and religious rights. The Left is assaulting those rights. We must resist this assault. Although our fight is spiritual, there is still much we can do in the physical realm.

In Rod Dreher's book *The Benedict Option: A Strategy for Christians in a Post-Christian Nation*, he discloses how Lance Kinzen, a ten-year Republican veteran of the Kansas state legislature, left his seat to promote religious liberty legislation in state houses across the country. Kinzer declares that religious liberty is our number one issue. He advises the church to:

- Send personal letters and meet face-to-face with lawmakers at the state and local level.
- Invite local media to cover the religious side in religious liberty issues.
- Form partnerships across denominations and even with non-Christians who support religious liberty.[112]

Spiritual Discipline: To stand for righteousness, one must lead a holy life, consecrating each day to God and obeying His decrees, especially those guarding the sacredness of sex.

Spiritual Gift: Those with the spiritual gift of encouragement can help those who have fallen sexually by urging them to repent and lead a life faithful to God's decrees.

Crown: The crown of righteousness (2 Timothy 4:8) will be given to those who are weary of the unrighteousness and lies so prevalent in today's world and long for Jesus to return.

SMART Goal Example: To stand for righteousness, by 8:00 a.m. today I will ask God to reveal any unrighteousness in my life. I will make a list and begin with one item on the list to overcome, confessing my sin to God and asking for forgiveness every time I commit that sin.

> If we confess our sins, he is faithful and just and will forgive us our sins and purify us from all unrighteousness. (1 John 1:9)

Feet Fitted with the Readiness that Comes from the Gospel of Peace

Roman Soldier's Weapon: A Roman soldier wore hobnail sandals (caligae) that gripped the ground and provided foot support and balance.

Christian's Weapon: The Christian's shoes represent a readiness to share the gospel through acts of service to unbelievers.

Use: We have the solution to the conflict in the world. We know how the world ends, and what is the outcome. Only Jesus can establish true peace. Therefore, Christians possess the key to world peace, the good news of the Gospel that Jesus died for our sins.

> How beautiful on the mountains are the feet of those who bring good news, who proclaim peace, who bring good tidings, who proclaim salvation, who say to Zion, "Your God reigns!" (Isaiah 52:7)

> And how can anyone preach unless they are sent? As it is written: "How beautiful are the feet of those who bring good news!" (Romans 10:15)

> Peace I [Jesus] leave with you; my peace I give you. I do not give to you as the world gives. Do not let your hearts be troubled and do not be afraid. (John 14:27)

Spiritual Discipline: To train for end times readiness, we can each participate in a service ministry, develop our personal testimony, and prepare to share it with unbelievers. During the time leading up to the rapture, society will continue to break down, providing opportunities for Christians to build bridges to hurting people. Separated from God, their lives will lack purpose, and they will face mounting despair. A service ministry can provide counsel and comfort, leading to opportunities to share the Gospel.

> But even if you should suffer for what is right, you are blessed. "Do not fear their threats; do not be frightened." But in your hearts revere Christ as Lord. Always be prepared to give an answer to everyone who asks you to give the reason for the hope that you have. But do this with gentleness and respect. (1 Peter 3:14–15)

Not only must we give our time in ministry, we must give our financial resources.

> Remember this: Whoever sows sparingly will also reap sparingly, and whoever sows generously will also reap generously. Each of you should give what you have decided in your heart to give, not reluctantly or under compulsion, for God loves a cheerful giver. (2 Corinthians 9:6–7)

Spiritual Gift: Those who have the spiritual gifts of service, mercy, and giving can build effective channels to provide spiritual and financial support to unbelievers who need the good news of the Gospel. Those who have the spiritual gift of evangelism can most effectively share the Gospel with other people in a nonthreatening manner.

Crown: The soul winner's crown (1 Thessalonians 2:19–20) in heaven will be given to those who lead others to Christ.

SMART Goal Example: To establish my readiness to share the Gospel, in one month I will select and volunteer for a service ministry.

Shield of Faith

Roman Soldier's Weapon: A Roman soldier carried a two-foot-wide by four-foot-long shield (scutum) for protection against visible threats (sword thrusts) or invisible threats (arrows). Sometimes the enemy launched flaming arrows to start fires amid an opposing army's base to cause panic.

Christian's Weapon: The Christian must use the shield of faith to protect from the enemy's flaming arrows.

Use: We must guard against ambush by strengthening our faith. Arrows are hard to see in the air. They can hit when least expected. The most painful flaming arrows come from coworkers, friends or family, people we like and admire who unexpectedly attack our beliefs:

> They sharpen their tongues like swords and aim cruel words like deadly arrows. They shoot from ambush at the innocent; they shoot suddenly, without fear. (Psalm 64:3–4)

Ambushes rupture relationships and terminate jobs, undermining our resolve and weakening our ministry. To protect against these flaming arrows, we need faith. The writer of Hebrews says:

> Now faith is confidence in what we hope for and assurance about what we do not see. (Hebrews 11:1)

Strength comes from faith in God:

> The Lord is my strength and my defense; he has become my salvation. He is my God, and I will praise him, my father's God, and I will exalt him. (Exodus 15:2)

God is with us:

> Have I not commanded you? Be strong and courageous. Do not be afraid; do not be discouraged, for the Lord your God will be with you wherever you go. (Joshua 1:9)

God will lift us up:

> But those who hope in the Lord will renew their strength. They will soar on wings like eagles; they will run and not grow weary, they will walk and not be faint. (Isaiah 40:31)

Spiritual Discipline: To strengthen our faith, we must practice several spiritual disciplines, such as confession, fellowship, worship, Bible study, prayer, and fasting:

- *Confession.* When we sin, we break our fellowship with the Holy Spirit. We must quickly confess our sin to restore that fellowship:

  > If we confess our sins, he is faithful and just and will forgive us our sins and purify us from all unrighteousness. (1 John 1:9)

- *Fellowship.* If the government shuts down churches, Christians must form their own house churches. During the Communist persecution of the Eastern bloc countries, those house churches became communities, then a network, and eventually a force to collapse the Communist regimes:

  > And let us consider how we may spur one another on toward love and good deeds, not giving up meeting together, as some are in the habit of doing, but encouraging one another—and all the more as you see the Day approaching. (Hebrews 10:24–25)

- *Worship.* To connect with God and draw upon His strength, we must praise His power and majesty:

  Come, let us sing for joy to the Lord; let us shout aloud to the Rock of our salvation. Let us come before him with thanksgiving and extol him with music and song. For the Lord is the great God, the great King above all gods. In his hand are the depths of the earth, and the mountain peaks belong to him. The sea is his, for he made it, and his hands formed the dry land. Come, let us bow down in worship, let us kneel before the Lord our Maker. (Psalm 95:1–6)

- *Bible study.* God's word, the Bible, grounds our faith. We must know and memorize the promises of God, our reassurance when ambushed:

  His divine power has given us everything we need for a godly life through our knowledge of him who called us by his own glory and goodness. Through these he has given us his very great and precious promises, so that through them you may participate in the divine nature, having escaped the corruption in the world caused by evil desires. (2 Peter 1:3–4)

- *Prayer.* When we are out in the field, we must establish a communications channel to "headquarters" for support and reinforcement. Prayer provides that link:

  Do not be anxious about anything, but in every situation, by prayer and petition, with thanksgiving, present your requests to God. (Philippians 4:6)

  Then Jesus told his disciples a parable to show them that they should always pray and not give up. (Luke 18:1)

- *Fasting.* We can also fast to seek guidance or deliverance. Fasting also promotes self-denial to prepare for future periods of extreme shortages:

> Alarmed, Jehoshaphat resolved to inquire of the Lord, and he proclaimed a fast for all Judah. The people of Judah came together to seek help from the Lord; indeed, they came from every town in Judah to seek him. (2 Chronicles 20:3–4)

Spiritual Gift: Those who have the gift of faith provide strength when circumstances seem hopeless. Those who have the gift of leadership provide hope in the midst of difficulty. Both gifts model courage, and courage is contagious.

Crown: The crown of life (James 1:12) in heaven will be given to those who endure trial, temptation, and persecution and stand firm with their shield of faith.

SMART Goal Example: To strengthen my faith, I will join or form a Bible study in thirty days, which can become my small group and future house church during severe persecution.

Helmet of Salvation

Roman Soldier's Weapon: The helmet (galea) of the Roman soldier protected his head. Once the head is injured, the soldier is defeated.

Christian's Weapon: The Christian's helmet is salvation, which is Jesus Christ. He can protect our minds. He can give us courage.

Use: We must remind ourselves that because of Jesus's death and resurrection, all things are possible.

> I can do all this through him who gives me strength. (Philippians 4:13)

What once was most fearful, death, is merely a gateway to a glorious new life.

> For God so loved the world that he gave his one and only Son, that whoever believes in him shall not perish but have eternal life. (John 3:16)

If death itself cannot intimidate us, why should anyone or anything do so? One way to become more courageous and bold is to share the Gospel with others. Not only will it remind us of our own salvation, it will through practice dispel the fear of rejection.

Spiritual Discipline: We all must practice the spiritual discipline of evangelism, sharing with unbelievers our personal testimony of coming to faith in Christ. All believers are equipped and required to do so. Therefore, have your personal testimony rehearsed and ready to share at a moment's notice.

Spiritual Gift: Some people are evangelist specialists equipped by the Holy Spirit (Ephesians 4:11) with a supernatural ability to share the Gospel with almost anyone in a nonthreatening way.

Crown: The soul winner's crown in heaven will be given to those who lead others to Jesus Christ.

SMART Goal Example: To become more courageous and bold, in seven days I will write my story of coming to faith in Christ and rehearse it several times. Then, I will pray for God to lead me to someone with whom I can share my testimony.

Sword of the Spirit

Roman Soldier's Weapon: The Roman soldier's sword (gladius) was twenty-four inches long and sharpened on both sides. Unlike a long sword that is sharpened on one side and must be swung, a soldier could thrust a more maneuverable short sword in close quarters.

Christian's Weapon: To maneuver in close quarters, the Christian must know the Word of God, the Bible.

Use: Knowing God's word deflects the lies of Satan when tempted:

> Jesus, full of the Holy Spirit, left the Jordan and was led by the Spirit into the wilderness, where for forty days he was tempted by the devil. He ate nothing during those days, and at the end of them he was hungry. The devil said to him, "If you are the Son of God, tell this stone to become bread." Jesus answered, "It is written: 'Man shall not live on bread alone.'" (Luke 4:1–4)

Sharing God's word penetrates a listener's innermost being:

> For the word of God is alive and active. Sharper than any double-edged sword, it penetrates even to dividing soul and spirit, joints and marrow; it judges the thoughts and attitudes of the heart. (Hebrews 4:12)

Using God's word accomplishes God's will:

> So is my word that goes out from my mouth: It will not return to me empty, but will accomplish what I desire and achieve the purpose for which I sent it. (Isaiah 55:11)

Using God's word, not our own, employs supernatural power:

> And so it was with me, brothers and sisters. When I came to you, I did not come with eloquence or human wisdom as I proclaimed to you the testimony about God. For I resolved to know nothing while I was with you except Jesus Christ and him crucified ... so that your faith might not rest on human wisdom, but on God's power. (1 Corinthians 2:1–2, 5)

Spiritual Discipline: To wield the Sword of the Spirit, the Word of God, during the end times, requires Bible knowledge and memorization.

Therefore, we must study the Bible daily. To recite a Bible verse from memory when speaking with unbelievers is more powerful than merely expressing our own opinion. As a backup, Bible verses printed on small cards are useful if our memory fails.

Spiritual Gift: The Holy Spirit will impart the spiritual gift of teaching and wisdom to specialists. This person is uniquely able to explain God's word in a way that people understand and to apply it to the issues of the day.

Crown: The victor's crown (1 Corinthians 9:24–25) is given in heaven to those who exercise self-discipline by studying the Bible and praying.

SMART Goal Example: To train using the Sword of the Spirit, the Word of God, in one month I will memorize all relevant Bible verses that explain the Gospel.

Conclusion

As hardship and persecution increases during the end times, and God's commandments about sexual behavior are attacked and censored, Christians must stand firm.

> Submit yourselves, then, to God. Resist the devil, and he will flee from you. Come near to God and he will come near to you. Wash your hands, you sinners, and purify your hearts, you double-minded. Grieve, mourn and wail. Change your laughter to mourning and your joy to gloom. Humble yourselves before the Lord, and he will lift you up. (James 4:7–10)

Circumstances will not be pleasant. Gone will be the freedoms and comforts we once enjoyed. Defeat, though, is not an option. We have God's weapons at our disposal. We must live not by lies. We must stand firm for the truth and against sexual sin.

As the world drifts further from God's truth, life will grow more meaningless for many. They will respond by seeking pleasure to numb their despair. We can offer an oasis of relief with the good news of the Gospel.

However, we must be alert. Expect ambushes from unexpected quarters. We must develop a strong faith grounded in Bible doctrine. Above all, we must be courageous and bold, fixing our gaze beyond the horizon to Jesus's glorious kingdom, which is the subject of the next chapter.

9

The Objective

While preparing to face the Mongolian horde, the city of Wroclaw will face obstacles. Defeatists will demand surrender. Building materials will disappear. Weapons won't work. Leaders will give conflicting orders, and tensions will boil over. To charge past those obstacles and finish their work, the citizens must concentrate on their objective. They must visualize what victory looks like. In their mind they must see the horde melting away and retreating to the east. To win, the citizens of Wroclaw must keep their objective in mind and not get distracted.

Training is never easy, as obstacles impede progress. To persevere in the midst of end times hardship and persecution, we also must visualize the objective, the rapture of the church—and avoidance of the tribulation with its horrific consequences. Secondarily, we must visualize the millennial kingdom that follows, and our ultimate destination, the new heaven and new earth, which is the finish line, our journey's end.

> Since, then, you have been raised with Christ, set your hearts on things above, where Christ is, seated at the right hand of God. Set your minds on things above, not on earthly things (Colossians 3:1–2)

Difficult circumstances must not rob us of our joy in life; we only have a short time on this earth. This chapter will help us live victoriously amidst any turmoil. Remember, this is not our best life now; the best is yet to come!

> God is our refuge and strength, an ever-present help in trouble. (Psalm 46:1)

Rapture

Because the rapture could occur at any time, it is our primary goal. After that, we can anticipate the millennial kingdom and new heaven and new earth. Therefore, we will begin our discussion with the rapture. The apostle Paul writes to Titus to wait for the "blessed hope" to come.

> It [grace of God] teaches us to say "No" to ungodliness
> and worldly passions, and to live self-controlled, upright
> and godly lives in this present age, while we wait for the
> blessed hope—the appearing of the glory of our great
> God and Savior, Jesus Christ. (Titus 2:12–13)

Our hope is the appearance of Jesus Christ in an instant, what Paul
called "the twinkling of an eye":

> Listen, I tell you a mystery: We will not all sleep, but
> we will all be changed— in a flash, in the twinkling of
> an eye, at the last trumpet. For the trumpet will sound,
> the dead will be raised imperishable, and we will be
> changed. (1 Corinthians 15:51–52)

The Lord will descend from heaven with a shout and the sound of
a trumpet. Those Christians who died previously will rise first. Then
the living believers will be "caught up." Therefore, all believers will meet
the Lord in the air and be taken to heaven.

> For the Lord himself will come down from heaven, with
> a loud command, with the voice of the archangel and
> with the trumpet call of God, and the dead in Christ
> will rise first. After that, we who are still alive and are
> left will be caught up together with them in the clouds
> to meet the Lord in the air. And so we will be with the
> Lord forever (1 Thessalonians 4:16–17)

Think of the implication. One generation of Christians will not die!
No casket, no funeral, no burial. In an instant, they will pass from life
on earth to life in heaven and come face to face with King Jesus. Imagine
the glorious reunion with relatives and friends who have previously died.

Remember the weightlessness you felt as a child when your parents
lifted you up or when you were suspended in midair at the top of a long
push on a swing set. Now visualize your Father in heaven lifting you
up from the earth. Feel the freedom, as the cares of this present age
melt away.

Remember the ad for Southwest Airlines: "Need to get away?" Well, the mother of all "get-aways" is the rapture.

Oh, by the way, this is not the first time that people were raptured. Enoch was raptured:

> By faith Enoch was taken from this life, so that he did not experience death: "He could not be found, because God had taken him away." For before he was taken, he was commended as one who pleased God. (Hebrews 11:5)

Elijah was raptured:

> As they were walking along and talking together, suddenly a chariot of fire and horses of fire appeared and separated the two of them, and Elijah went up to heaven in a whirlwind. (2 Kings 2:11)

Neither Enoch nor Elijah died. That is the way to go! *That* is something to look forward to.

Also—and this is a big also—we will not have to face the "coming wrath" of God through the tribulation. Paul wrote:

> And to wait for his Son from heaven, whom he raised from the dead—Jesus, who rescues us from the coming wrath. (1 Thessalonians 1:10)

> For God did not appoint us to suffer wrath but to receive salvation through our Lord Jesus Christ. (1 Thessalonians 5:9)

In Jesus's letter to the Philadelphia church, He promised to keep them from "the hour of trial":

> Since you have kept my command to endure patiently, I will also keep you from the hour of trial that is going to

come on the whole world to test the inhabitants of the earth. (Revelation 3:10)

So, even though times will get tougher, there are much, much tougher times coming, which we can avoid. We must keep our eyes on the prize, the rapture of the church.

Difference between Rapture and Second Coming

Throughout history people have confused the rapture with the second coming. If you compare the accounts of the rapture in 1 Thessalonians 4 and 1 Corinthians 15 with the accounts of the second coming in Matthew 24 and 25, you can detect the key differences, as displayed in Table 3. Difference between the Rapture and Second Coming.

Difference between the Rapture and Second Coming		
Difference	Rapture	Second Coming
Jesus's destination	Jesus comes in the air and does not touch down. "After that, we who are still alive and are left will be caught up together with them in the clouds to meet the Lord in the air. And so we will be with the Lord forever." (1 Thessalonians 4:17)	Jesus sits on His throne on earth. "When the Son of Man comes in his glory, and all the angels with him, he will sit on his glorious throne. All the nations will be gathered before him, and he will separate the people one from another as a shepherd separates the sheep from the goats." (Matthew 25:31–32)
Humanity's destination	Dead and living believers rise and are united with Christ. "For the Lord himself will come down from heaven, with a loud command, with the voice of the archangel and with the trumpet call of God, and the dead in Christ will rise first. After that, we who are still alive and are left will be caught up together with them in the clouds to meet the Lord in the air. And so we will be with the Lord forever." (1 Thessalonians 4:16–17)	Living unbelievers are separated from Christ. "He will put the sheep on his right and the goats on his left ... Then he will say to those on his left, 'Depart from me, you who are cursed, into the eternal fire prepared for the devil and his angels.'" (Matthew 25:33, 41)

Difference between the Rapture and Second Coming		
Difference	Rapture	Second Coming
Duration	In an instant	Long enough to see and mourn
	"Listen, I tell you a mystery: We will not all sleep, but we will all be changed—in a flash, in the twinkling of an eye, at the last trumpet. For the trumpet will sound, the dead will be raised imperishable, and we will be changed." (1 Corinthians 15:51–52)	"Then will appear the sign of the Son of Man in heaven. And then all the peoples of the earth will mourn when they see the Son of Man coming on the clouds of heaven, with power and great glory." (Matthew 24:30)

Table 3. Difference between the Rapture and Second Coming

Millennial Kingdom

The millennial kingdom follows the rapture and tribulation and promises to be spectacular. The second coming of Jesus ushers in His one-thousand-year millennial kingdom. After all, Christians have prayed about the millennial kingdom for thousands of years when uttering the words of the Lord's prayer:

> This, then, is how you should pray: "Our Father in heaven, hallowed be your name, **your kingdom come**, your will be done, on earth as it is in heaven." (Matthew 6:9–10)(emphasis added)

Satan, the father of all deception and evil, is absent during this 1,000-year period:

> And I saw an angel coming down out of heaven, having the key to the Abyss and holding in his hand a great chain. He seized the dragon, that ancient serpent, who is the devil, or Satan, and bound him for a thousand years. He threw him into the Abyss, and locked and sealed it over him, to keep him from deceiving the nations anymore until the thousand years were ended. After that, he must be set free for a short time. (Revelation 20:1–3)

Since the principle evil force in the world is inactive during this period, fake news, half-truths, and clever lies disappear as well.

Who Is Present During the Millennial Kingdom? Present during the millennial kingdom are the raptured church, the saints killed during the tribulation, and the believers, both Jewish and Gentile, who survive the tribulation.

When Jesus returns, so will His faithful followers, the raptured church:

> They will wage war against the Lamb, but the Lamb will triumph over them because he is Lord of lords and King of kings—and with him will be his called, chosen and faithful followers. (Revelation 17:14)

> The armies of heaven were following him, riding on white horses and dressed in fine linen, white and clean. (Revelation 19:14)

Who is this army dressed in fine linen, white and clean? The following verse refers to them as the "bride" of Christ (the church), who wear "fine linen, bright and clean."

> Then I heard what sounded like a great multitude, like the roar of rushing waters and like loud peals of thunder, shouting: "Hallelujah! For our Lord God Almighty reigns. Let us rejoice and be glad and give him glory! For the wedding of the Lamb has come, and his bride has made herself ready. Fine linen, bright and clean, was given her to wear." (Fine linen stands for the righteous acts of God's holy people.) (Revelation 19:6–8)

Lastly, those believers who were executed for their faith during the tribulation are resurrected during the millennial kingdom:

> I saw thrones on which were seated those who had been given authority to judge. And I saw the souls of those who had been beheaded because of their testimony

about Jesus and because of the word of God. They had not worshiped the beast or its image and had not received its mark on their foreheads or their hands. They came to life and reigned with Christ a thousand years. (Revelation 20:4)

Who Rules in the Millennial Kingdom? Jesus will rule from Jerusalem:

> For to us a child is born, to us a son is given, and the government will be on his shoulders. And he will be called Wonderful Counselor, Mighty God, Everlasting Father, Prince of Peace. Of the greatness of his government and peace there will be no end. He will reign on David's throne and over his kingdom, establishing and upholding it with justice and righteousness from that time on and forever. The zeal of the Lord Almighty will accomplish this. (Isaiah 9:6–7)

> You will conceive and give birth to a son, and you are to call him Jesus. He will be great and will be called the Son of the Most High. The Lord God will give him the throne of his father David, and he will reign over Jacob's descendants forever; his kingdom will never end. (Luke 1:31–33)

What Will Life Be Like in the Millennial Kingdom?

Peace. There will be peace in the world.

> He [the Lord] will judge between the nations and will settle disputes for many peoples. They will beat their swords into plowshares and their spears into pruning hooks. Nation will not take up sword against nation, nor will they train for war anymore. (Isaiah 2:4)

Prosperity. People will rejoice because their needs are satisfied. There is an abundance of everything and therefore no want, hunger or thirst.

> "They will come and shout for joy on the heights of Zion; they will rejoice in the bounty of the Lord—the grain, the new wine and the olive oil, the young of the flocks and herds. They will be like a well-watered garden, and they will sorrow no more. Then young women will dance and be glad, young men and old as well. I will turn their mourning into gladness; I will give them comfort and joy instead of sorrow. I will satisfy the priests with abundance, and my people will be filled with my bounty," declares the Lord. (Jeremiah 31:12–14)

Righteousness. All people will know the difference between right and wrong.

> For the earth will be filled with the knowledge of the glory of the Lord as the waters cover the sea. (Habakkuk 2:14)

Imagine a life with peace, prosperity, and unity, with Jesus king over all for one-thousand years. Plenty of time to visit those places on earth you've always wanted to see, although likely altered by the tribulation. Plenty of time to visit and get reacquainted with relatives. However, as good as it is during the millennial kingdom, the best is yet to come.

Heaven

After the millennial kingdom, God will transform the universe back to what He originally intended. He revealed His plans through the prophet Isaiah:

> See, I will create new heavens and a new earth. The former things will not be remembered, nor will they come to mind. (Isaiah 65:17)

Heaven and earth will merge, because God's residence is called heaven, and He will dwell with His people.

> Then I saw "a new heaven and a new earth," for the first heaven and the first earth had passed away, and there was no longer any sea. I saw the Holy City, the new Jerusalem, coming down out of heaven from God, prepared as a bride beautifully dressed for her husband. And I heard a loud voice from the throne saying, "Look! God's dwelling place is now among the people, and he will dwell with them. They will be his people, and God himself will be with them and be their God." (Revelation 21:1–3)

We can expect a new and improved earth with certain territories preserved, such as the land of Canaan, which God gave to the children of Israel as an everlasting possession:

> I will establish my covenant as an everlasting covenant between me and you and your descendants after you for the generations to come, to be your God and the God of your descendants after you. The whole land of Canaan, where you now reside as a foreigner, I will give as an everlasting possession to you and your descendants after you; and I will be their God. (Genesis 17:7–8)

Terrain in Heaven

The new heaven and new earth will likely have familiar terrain, with mountains, rivers, trees, houses, and cities. We are provided details about a specific city, New Jerusalem:

> It shone with the glory of God, and its brilliance was like that of a very precious jewel, like a jasper, clear as crystal.

> The city was laid out like a square, as long as it was wide. He measured the city with the rod and found it to be 12,000 stadia in length, and as wide and high as it is long. The angel measured the wall using human measurement, and it was 144 cubits thick. The wall was made of jasper, and the city of pure gold, as pure as glass. The foundations of the city walls were decorated with every kind of precious stone.

> The city does not need the sun or the moon to shine on it, for the glory of God gives it light, and the Lamb is its lamp. (Revelation 21:11, 16–19a, 23)

According to the modern equivalents of the measures in Revelation 21, the city is 1,400 miles, long, wide, and high. Placed in the center of the United States, the city would stretch north to Canada, south to Mexico, east to the Appalachian Mountains, and west to the California border. Billions of people could live there with plenty of space for everybody.

The city glows with the glory of God, producing a warm golden light, like that streaming from the windows of your home at night. Imagine such a place: the sky bluer than anything you have seen; the grass softer than anything you have touched; the flowers sweeter than anything you have smelled. Imagine soaring mountains, expansive valleys, and glittering cities, beyond anything we can imagine.

> However, as it is written: "What no eye has seen, what no ear has heard, and what no human mind has conceived"—the things God has prepared for those who love him. (1 Corinthians 2:9)

We Will Have Resurrection Bodies like Jesus

In heaven there is no death, no disability, and no deterioration. Our resurrected bodies will be like Jesus's body after His resurrection:

> Who, by the power that enables him to bring everything under his control, will transform our lowly bodies so that they will be like his glorious body. (Philippians 3:21)

Our resurrected bodies will not wear out.

> There are also heavenly bodies and there are earthly bodies; but the splendor of the heavenly bodies is one kind, and the splendor of the earthly bodies is another. The sun has one kind of splendor, the moon another and the stars another; and star differs from star in splendor. So will it be with the resurrection of the dead. The body that is sown is perishable, it is raised imperishable; it is sown in dishonor, it is raised in glory; it is sown in weakness, it is raised in power; it is sown a natural body, it is raised a spiritual body. If there is a natural body, there is also a spiritual body. (1 Corinthians 15:40–44)

We will not be constrained by physical limits. For example, after stopping at a follower's house in Emmaus, Jesus disappeared.

> When he was at the table with them, he took bread, gave thanks, broke it and began to give it to them. Then their eyes were opened and they recognized him, and he disappeared from their sight. They asked each other, "Were not our hearts burning within us while he talked with us on the road and opened the Scriptures to us?" (Luke 24:30–32)

Later, Jesus reappeared suddenly among His disciples in Jerusalem, about seven miles from Emmaus.

> While they were still talking about this, Jesus himself stood among them and said to them, "Peace be with you." They were startled and frightened, thinking they saw a ghost. He said to them, "Why are you troubled, and why do doubts rise in your minds? Look at my

hands and my feet. It is I myself! Touch me and see; a ghost does not have flesh and bones, as you see I have." When he had said this, he showed them his hands and feet. (Luke 24:36–40)

Jesus's body was physical to the touch, yet spiritual. The physical properties permitted Him to eat food:

And while they still did not believe it because of joy and amazement, he asked them, "Do you have anything here to eat?" They gave him a piece of broiled fish, and he took it and ate it in their presence. (Luke 24:41–43)

That's important because we don't want to miss an important banquet in heaven:

Then the angel said to me, "Write this: Blessed are those who are invited to the wedding supper of the Lamb!" And he added, "These are the true words of God." (Revelation 19:9)

Most significantly, we will live in the presence of God and gratefully serve our Lord and King, the One who loves us unconditionally.

Conclusion

There is much to look forward to, much to divert our attention from any suffering, frustration, and sorrow we may experience as we live through the end times.

So we fix our eyes not on what is seen, but on what is unseen, since what is seen is temporary, but what is unseen is eternal. (2 Corinthians 4:18)

We can bypass death through the rapture and avoid the terrible tribulation and judgment of God. We can triumphantly return to earth with Jesus for one thousand years and enjoy a time of peace, prosperity, and righteousness. Finally, we can inhabit the new heaven and new earth, with familiar terrain, only brought up to God's perfect standards. We will live forever with God, our Hero and King, and will daily experience His incomparable love.

> And I pray that you, being rooted and established in love, may have power, together with all the Lord's holy people, to grasp how wide and long and high and deep is the love of Christ, and to know this love that surpasses knowledge—that you may be filled to the measure of all the fullness of God. (Ephesians 3:17b–19)

10

The Consequence of Failure

If the citizens of Wroclaw do not adequately prepare to defend their city from the Golden Horde, the result will be chaos and defeat. A half-hearted defense will only instigate the Mongols to try harder. They will sense weakness and press for the kill. By the way, the Mongols like to collect the ears of their victims in sacks as keepsakes. To bring victory, the city must plan, prepare, and unite behind a common goal. They must make the defense of their city so dear to the enemy that the Golden Horde will break down and quit.

What are the consequences of failure for us? Imagine that the apostle James had written an open letter to the United States addressing our deep divide:

> What causes fights and quarrels among you? Don't they come from your desires that battle within you? (James 4:1)

Sexual desires have caused a battle within our nation: sex before marriage, sex visualized with pornography, sex between men and sex between women, and sex change operations.

> You desire but do not have, so you kill. (James 4:2a)

Women desire sex, like men, without the consequences, so women abort their babies.

> You covet but you cannot get what you want, so you quarrel and fight. (James 4:2b)

The poor covet what the rich have. The Left denounces the top 1 percent of the rich and cry for a more socialist government to take from the rich and give to the poor. The Left drives a wedge between groups and agitates one group to overpower the other.

> You do not have because you do not ask God. When you ask, you do not receive, because you ask with wrong motives, that you may spend what you get on your pleasures. (James 4:2c–3)

The poor seek help from the government, not from God. They spend money on drugs, alcohol, and entertainment to blunt their alienation from God. They have sex without marriage and try to raise children within one-parent households.

> You adulterous people, don't you know that friendship with the world means enmity against God? Therefore, anyone who chooses to be a friend of the world becomes an enemy of God. (James 4:4)

We have revealed how once our country respected the Bible and lived by its commandments but now disassociates itself from any connection to biblical truth. We have reviewed the many fulfilled prophecies of the Bible; the Bible indeed predicts the future and is 100 percent accurate. We have disclosed the important prophecies yet to be fulfilled and the awful judgments intended for those who reject Christ. We have traced our country's steady slide into sexual sin and the consequent judgments of God. We have warned that time is short, and we must prepare for the coming persecution before the tribulation. Lastly, we have provided the blessed hope we have in the rapture, millennial kingdom, and new heaven and new earth.

Now we ask, what is the consequence of failure to prepare for the end times? The first question to ask is: will you be left behind to face the tribulation, with its hideous pestilence, tyranny, and bloodshed, or will you be saved?

There is only one way to be saved. It is through Jesus Christ, who proclaimed,

> "I am the way and the truth and the life. No one comes to the Father except through me." (John 14:6)

How to Be Saved

So, how does a person come to the Father through Jesus? How can a person be saved? Think of it as a three-step process that the great evangelist Billy Graham offered to more than 215 million people around the world who attended his more than four hundred crusades:

One. Admit you are a sinner and need a savior. We are all sinners and cannot enter God's sin-free environment:

> For all have sinned and fall short of the glory of God. (Romans 3:23)

There is a gulf between us and God that we cannot bridge on our own. Left to ourselves, we face judgment and eternal separation from God, as displayed in Figure 3. Man Is Separated from God.

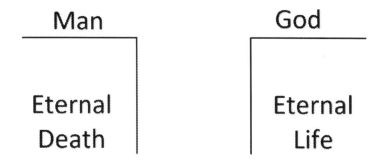

Figure 3. Man Is Separated from God

Two. Repent. Change your attitude and the direction of your life by turning away from your sins, as Jesus revealed:

> "It is not the healthy who need a doctor, but the sick. I have not come to call the righteous, but sinners to repentance." (Luke 5:31–32)

Three. Believe that Jesus died for your sins and was raised from the dead:

> For God so loved the world that he gave his one and only Son, that whoever believes in him shall not perish but have eternal life. (John 3:16)

Jesus is the only way to heaven. There is no other way. Believing you are a good person won't work. Believing in Buddha or Mohammed won't work. Only believing in Jesus's death and resurrection will work. This is displayed in Figure 4.

> Jesus answered, "I am the way and the truth and the life. No one comes to the Father except through me." (John 14:6)

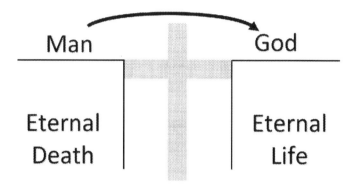

Figure 4. Man Is Reconciled to God

Good News

- Men and women are sinners—we are born into sin.
- God the Father cannot tolerate sin.
- However, God loves you and wants you to be with Him in heaven.
- God sent His only Son, Jesus, to pay the debt for your sins.
- Only Jesus, who is God, can pay this debt.
- He died on the cross for your sins.
- He rose from the dead three days later.
- You need to repent of your sins and trust in Jesus as your Savior.

God loves you so much that He gave His only Son, Jesus Christ, to die for your sins. If you believe in Him, turn from your sins, and make Jesus the Lord of your life, you will have eternal life with Him in Heaven. That is the way to avoid the terrible consequences of the tribulation.

Will You Pray This Prayer Today?

Dear God,

I know I'm a sinner, and I ask for your forgiveness. I believe Jesus Christ is Your Son. I believe that He died for my sin and that you raised Him to life. I want to trust Him as my Savior and follow Him as Lord, from this day forward. Guide my life and help me to do your will. I pray this in the name of Jesus. Amen.

———————————   ———————————
Date   Signature

If you have prayed this prayer and accepted Jesus Christ into your life by faith, please contact us at TrainingGuideMinistry.com. Live your life with the end in mind, so that your last breath on earth will be your first breath in heaven.

Once you are saved, however, the second question to ask is: will you use the spiritual weapons described in this book to live courageously during the days that lead up to the rapture? The alternative is a life battered by waves of anxiety and despair with each passing government edict or headline in the news. The choice is yours.

Conclusion

Defeat is not an option. We still have Constitutional rights to exercise in this country. If those are revoked, then we wage a fighting retreat. However, our weapons and foes are spiritual. We will need a persevering spirit, like that of the First Marine Division of the X Corp at the Battle of Chosin Reservoir in North Korea, November to December 1950.

During a brutally cold winter in mountainous terrain, the division, around 30,000 Marines, were surprised, attacked, and surrounded by 120,000 Chinese soldiers. Rather than surrender, the Marines fought their way out, at times battling down narrow roads through the mountains. On both sides of the passes the enemy focused their fire at the truck drivers transporting the troops. Surrounded at Hagaru-ri, the Marines had to construct a landing strip while under fire to allow planes to fly in ammunition and supplies. As they resumed their march, they also had to rebuild a destroyed bridge while under fire at Funchilin Pass.

Step-by-step they mounted a fighting retreat. Small groups of marines would defend strategic hills to allow the main body to pass by. For example, Captain William E. Barber, commanding company F, defended such a hilltop. Completely surrounded by an overwhelming enemy force, Company F held on for five days and six nights with little sleep, frozen food, and unremitting fanatical assaults by the enemy. Barber was severely wounded in the leg and moved about by stretcher to direct the defense and encourage his men until the main body of the Marines extricated them.

Barber's defense helped save the Marines, who eventually marched to safety, along with their equipment, to the coastal city of Hungnam, on the Sea of Japan, where they were relieved by ship.

We too must possess the courage and tenacity of Captain Barber, although our weapons are spiritual, and our foe attacks in the spiritual realm. We too are here to save a remnant. We too must do our duty until relieved by Jesus.

Now is the time to persevere and live victoriously.

Whoever dwells in the shelter of the Most High will rest in the shadow of the Almighty. I will say of the Lord, "He is my refuge and my fortress, my God, in whom I trust." Surely he will save you from the fowler's snare and from the deadly pestilence. He will cover you with his feathers, and under his wings you will find refuge; his faithfulness will be your shield and rampart. You will not fear the terror of night, nor the arrow that flies by day, nor the pestilence that stalks in the darkness, nor the plague that destroys at midday. A thousand may fall at your side, ten thousand at your right hand, but it will not come near you. You will only observe with your eyes and see the punishment of the wicked.

— Psalm 91:1–8

Endnotes

1. Grant, G., "Alexander's Siege of Tyre, 332 BCE," *Ancient History Encyclopedia*, August 8 2011, accessed February 16, 2021, https://www.ancient.eu/article/107/alexanders-siege-of-tyre-332-bce/.

2. Cartwright, M., "The Mongol Invasion of Europe," *World History Encyclopedia*, October 2, 2019, Accessed December 2, 2021, https://www.worldhistory.org/article/1453/the-mongol-invasion-of-europe/.

3. Religion News, "SHOCK POLL: Startling Numbers of Americans Believe World Now in the 'End Times'," *Religion News Service*, September 11, 2013, Accessed November 3, 2021, https://religionnews.com/2013/09/11/shock-poll-startling-numbers-of-americans-believe-world-now-in-the-end-times/.

4. The Avalon Project, "The First Charter of Virginia; April 10, 1606," *Lillian Goldman Law Library*, accessed March 11, 2021, https://avalon.law.yale.edu/17th_century/va01.asp#1.

5. Plimoth Plantation, "Mayflower and Mayflower Compact," *Plimoth Plantation*, accessed March 11, 2021, https://www.plimoth.org/learn/just-kids/homework-help/mayflower-and-mayflower-compact.

6. The Avalon Project, "Constitution of Delaware; 1776," *Lillian Goldman Law Library*, accessed March 11, 2021, https://avalon.law.yale.edu/18th_century/de02.asp.

7. McGuffey, W. H., "Lesson XX: John Jones," in *The Eclectic First Reader for You Children with Pictures*. Cinninatti: Truman and Smith, 1836, 57-59.

8. Webster, N., "Marriage," *American Dictionary of the English Language*, accessed March 16, 2021, http://webstersdictionary1828.com/Dictionary/marriage.

9. Harvard University, "Harvard GSAS Christian Community," *Harvard GSAS Christian Community*, [Online], accessed March 17, 2021, http://www.hcs.harvard.edu/~gsascf/shield-and-veritas-history/.

10. Christianity Today, "George Whitefield," *Christianity Today*, accessed March 13, 2021, https://www.christianitytoday.com/history/people/evangelistsandapologists/george-whitefield.html.

11. Franklin, B., "The Autobiography," in *The Autobiography and Selected Writings*, New York: The Modern Library, 1950, 118.

12. Finney, C. G. "The Gospel Truth: The Memoirs of Charles G. Finney," *Charlesgfinney.com*, accessed March 13, 2021, https://www.charlesgfinney.com/memoirsrestored/memrest21.htm.

13. Encyclopaedia Britannica, "Second Great Awakening," *Encyclopaedia Britannica,* accessed March 29, 2021, https://www.britannica.com/topic/Second-Great-Awakening.

14. Christianity Today, "Dwight L. Moody," *Christianity Today*, accessed September 25, 2021, https://www.christianitytoday.com/history/people/evangelistsandapologists/dwight-l-moody.html.

15. Got Questions Ministries, "Who was Billy Sunday?," *Got Questions Ministries*, accessed September 25, 2021, https://www.gotquestions.org/Billy-Sunday.html.

16. Billy Graham Evangelistic Association, "Official Obituary," *Billy Graham Evangelistic Association*, February 21, 2018, accessed September 25, 2021, https://memorial.billygraham.org/official-obituary/.

17. Shelley, M., "Evangelist Billy Graham Has Died," *Christianity Today*, accessed September 25, 2021, https://www.christianitytoday.com/ct/2018/billy-graham/.

18. Barna, "Signs of Decline & Hope Among Key Metrics of Faith," *Barna*, March 4, 2020, accessed March 29, 2021, https://www.barna.com/research/changing-state-of-the-church/.

19. Barna, "How We Got Here: Spiritual and Political Profiles of America," *Barna*, May 23, 2017, accessed March 29, 2021, https://www.barna.com/research/got-spiritual-political-profiles-america/.

20. Burgess, S., "Humans: Purposely Designed," *Answers in Genisis*, July 1, 2007, accessed February 17, 2021, https://answersingenesis.org/what-is-the-meaning-of-life/humans-purposely-designed/.

21. Paturi, J., "The Human Body-God's Masterpiece," *Answers in Genesis*, September 1, 1998, accessed February 17, 2021, https://answersingenesis.org/kids/anatomy/the-human-body/.

22. Muncaster, R. O., *101 Reasons You Can Believe: Why the Christian Faith Makes Sense*, Eugene, OR: Harvest House Publishers, 2004, 113.

23. Dorling Kindersley Limited, "Brain and nerves," *Dorling Kindersley Limited*, accessed February 17, 2021, https://www.dkfindout.com/us/human-body/brain-and-nerves/.

24. Cleveland Clinic, "How Does Blood Flow Through Your Body," *Cleveland Clinic*, accessed February 17, 2021, https://my.clevelandclinic.org/health/articles/17059-how-does-blood-flow-through-your-body.

25. McDowell, Josh and McDowell, Sean, *Evidence That Demands a Verdict: Life-Changing Truth for a Skeptical World.* Nashville: Thomas Nelson, 2017, 52.

26. Gleghorn, M., "Ancient Evidence for Jesus from Non-Christian Sources," *Probe Ministries*, August 30, 2014, accessed February 18, 2021, https://probe.org/ancient-evidence-for-jesus-from-non-christian-sources-2/#text5.

27. Frantzman, S., "Fallout from the Turkey-Iran-Russia meeting," *The Jerusalem Post*, April 6, 2018, accessed March 4, 2020, https://www.jpost.com/International/Fallout-from-the-Turkey-Iran-Russia-meeting-549022.

28. Sharon, J., "Temple-ready altar dedicated on last day of Hanukkah by activist groups," *The Jerusalem Post*, December 10. 2018, accessed January 16, 2020, https://www.jpost.com/Israel-News/Temple-ready-altar-dedicated-on-last-day-of-Hanukkah-by-activist-groups-573980.

29. Berkowitz, A., "Red Heifer Birth, Paves Way for Renewed Temple Service," *Israel365 News*, September 5, 2018, accessed December 3, 2020, https://www.israel365news.com/113476/temple-institute-certifies-red-heifer/.

30. Bas-Wohlert, C., "Microchips get under the skin of technophile Swedes," *Phys.org*, May 13, 2018, accessed January 16, 2020, https://phys.org/news/2018-05-microchips-skin-technophile-swedes.html.

31. Sawhill, I., "Marriage and Child Wellbeing Revisited:," *Princeton-Brookings*, 25, no. 2 (2015), accessed April 12, 2021, https://futureofchildren.princeton.edu/sites/futureofchildren/files/media/marriage_and_child_wellbeing_revisited_25_2_full_journal.pdf.

32. Wilcox, W. Bradford, Lerman, Robert I. and Price, Joseph, "Mobility and money in U.S. states: The marriage effect," *The Brookings Institution*, December 7, 2015, accessed April 12, 2021, https://www.brookings.edu/research/mobility-and-money-in-u-s-states-the-marriage-effect/.

33. Mohler, R. Albert, "Why the Sexual Revolution Needed a Sexual Revolutionary," *The Atlantic*, August 23, 2012, accessed July 26, 2019, https://www.theatlantic.com/entertainment/archive/2012/08/why-the-sexual-revolution-needed-a-sexual-revolutionary/261492/.

34. Golden, S., "Feminism: The Influence of Postmodernism," *Answers in Genesis*, March 13, 2013, accessed June 30, 2019, https://answersingenesis.org/family/gender/the-influence-of-postmodernism-part-5-feminism/.

35. Bergman, J., "Birth control leader Margaret Sanger: Darwinist, racist and eugenicist," *Creation Ministries International*, accessed July 27, 2019, https://creation.com/margaret-sanger-darwinian-eugenicist.

36. Whelan, E., "This Day in Liberal Judicial Activism—June 7," *National Review*, June 7, 2019, accessed July 11, 2019, https://www.nationalreview.com/bench-memos/this-day-in-liberal-judicial-activism-june-7-2/.

37. Kupelian, D., *The Marketing of Evil: How Radicals, Elitists, and Pseudo-Experts Sell Us Corruption Disguised as Freedom*, Nashville: WND Books, 2005.

38. Dorman, S., "An estimated 62 million abortions have occurred since Roe v. Wade decision in 1973," *Fox News*, January 22, 2021, accessed April 12, 2021, https://www.foxnews.com/politics/abortions-since-roe-v-wade.

39. Galvin, G., "U.S. Births Continue to Fall, Fertility Rate Hits Record Low," *U.S. News & World Report*, May 20, 2020, accessed April 12, 2021, https://www.usnews.com/news/healthiest-communities/articles/2020-05-20/us-births-continue-to-fall-fertility-rate-hits-record-low.

40. Wilcox, W. B., "The Evolution of Divorce," *National Affairs*, Fall 2009, accessed May 23, 2019, https://www.nationalaffairs.com/publications/detail/the-evolution-of-divorce.

41. American Sociological Association, "Women More Likely Than Men to Initiate Divorces, But Not Non-Marital Breakups," *American Sociological Association*, August 22, 2015, accessed April 12, 2021, https://www.asanet.org/press-center/press-releases/women-more-likely-men-initiate-divorces-not-non-marital-breakups.

42. Cruz, J., "Marriage: More Than a Century of Change," *National Center for Family & Marriage Research*, 2013, accessed April 12, 2021, https://www.bgsu.edu/content/dam/BGSU/college-of-arts-and-sciences/NCFMR/documents/FP/FP-13-13.pdf.

43. Child Trends, "Births to Unmarried Women," *Child Trends*, December 2015, accessed April 12, 2021, https://www.childtrends.org/wp-content/uploads/2015/03/75_Births_to_Unmarried_Women.pdf.

44. Reisman, J., "Kinsey and the Homosexual Revolution," *Journal of Human Sexuality*, 1996, accessed December 24, 2019, http://www.drjudithreisman.com/archives/2019/01/kinsey_and_the.html.

45. Gallop, "Gay and Lesbian Rights," *Gallop*, accessed July 24, 2020, https://news.gallup.com/poll/1651/gay-lesbian-rights.aspx.

46. Crain, C., "Alfred Kinsey: Liberator or Pervert?," *The New York Times*, October 3, 2004, accessed August 1, 2020, https://www.nytimes.com/2004/10/03/movies/alfred-kinsey-liberator-or-pervert.html.

47. Arkes, H., "Sodomy & The Law," *National Review*, July 2, 2003, accessed July 12, 2019, https://www.nationalreview.com/2003/07/sodomy-law-hadley-arkes/.

48. Hendershott, A., "The House of Lies," *The Catholic World Report*, March 26, 2013, accessed July 29, 2019, Available: https://www.catholicworldreport.com/2013/03/26/the-house-of-lies/.

49. Bradley, G. V., "Stand and Fight," *National Review*, July 12, 2004, accessed July 12, 2019, https://www.nationalreview.com/2004/07/stand-and-fight-gerard-v-bradley/.

50. Rosenfeld, M. J., "Moving a Mountain: The Extraordinary Trajectory of Same-Sex Marriage Approval in the United States," *Socius: Sociological Research for a Dynamic World*, September 15, 2017, accessed July 27, 2020, https://journals.sagepub.com/doi/full/10.1177/2378023117727658.

51. Rondeau, P. E., "Selling Homosexuality to American," *Regent University Law Review*, 2001-2002, accessed December 26, 2019, https://www.regent.edu/acad/schlaw/student_life/studentorgs/lawreview/docs/issues/v14n2/Vol.%2014,%20No.%202,%208%20Rondeau.pdf.

52. Mohler, A. "After the Ball—Why the Homosexual Movement Has Won," *Albertmohler.com*, June 3, 2004, accessed July 13, 2010, https://albertmohler.com/2004/06/03/after-the-ball-why-the-homosexual-movement-has-won.

53. Kirk, Marshall. &. Madsen, Hunter, *After the Ball: How America Will Conquer its Fear and Hatred of Gays in the 90s*, New York: Doubleday, 1989, 147-157.

54. Human Rights Campaign, "Corporate Equality Index," *Human Rights Campaign*, accessed July 29, 2020, https://www.hrc.org/campaigns/corporate-equality-index.

55. Socarides, C. W., "How America Went Gay," *The Road to Emmaus*, accessed July 15, 2020, https://theroadtoemmaus.org/RdLb/22SxSo/PnSx/HSx/SocrdsHowAmerGay.htm.

56. Hattaway Communications, "Changing The Dynamics Of A Controversial Issue," *Hattaway Communications*, accessed September 23, 2020, http://www.hattaway.com/stories/marriage-equality.

57. Totenberg, N., "Ted Olson, Gay Marriage's Unlikely Legal Warrior," *NPR*, December 6, 2010, accessed September 23, 2020, https://www.npr.org/2010/12/06/131792296/ted-olson-gay-marriage-s-unlikely-legal-warrior.

58. Last, J. V., "The Big, Fat, Gay Marriage Post-Mortem," *Weekly Standard*, July 1, 2015, accessed July 12, 2019, https://www.weeklystandard.com/jonathan-v-last/the-big-fat-gay-marriage-post-mortem.

59. Roberts, J., "Dissenting Opinion of Chief Justice John C. Roberts in Obergefell v Hodges," *Medium*, June 26, 2015, accessed July 28, 2019, https://medium.com/@e/dissenting-opinion-of-justice-john-c-roberts-f5e2ab4f1349.

60. Dallas, J., "The Transsexual Dilemma: A Dialogue About the Ethics of Sex Change," *Christian Research Institute*, 2008, accessed September 26, 2019, http://www.equip.org/PDF/JAT106.pdf.

61. Barna, G., "New Insights into the Generation of Growing Influence: Millennials," *Cultural Research Center at Arizona Christian University*, October

2021, accessed November 24, 2021, https://www.arizonachristian.edu/wp-content/uploads/2021/10/George-Barna-Millennial-Report-2021-FINAL-Web.pdf?.

62. Jeremiah, D., *Is This the End?*, Nashville:,W Publishing Group, 2016, 102.

63. Jeremiah, D., *Is This the End?*, 102-105.

64. MacArthur, J., "When God Abandons a Nation," *Grace to You*, August 20, 2006, accessed January 30, 2020, https://www.gty.org/library/sermons-library/80-314/when-god-abandons-a-nation.

65. Perry, M. J., "Michael Crichton in 2003: Environmentalism is a religion," *American Enterprise Institute*, April 17, 2019, accessed January 30, 2020, https://www.aei.org/carpe-diem/michael-chrichton-in-2003-environmentalism-is-a-religion/.

66. Dobnik, V., "New York court to determine if chimp is legally a person," *Associated Press*, March 16, 2017, accessed November 10, 2021, https://apnews.com/article/us-news-ap-top-news-manhattan-chimpanzees-oddities-b7aa70253e30433a92a1a61395c34749.

67. Hains, T., "Ocasio-Cortez: "The World Is Going To End In 12 Years If We Don't Address Climate Change"," *RealClear Politics*, January 22, 2019, accessed January 30, 2020, https://www.realclearpolitics.com/video/2019/01/22/ocasio-cortez_the_world_is_going_to_end_in_12_years_if_we_dont_address_climate_change.html.

68. Goodkind, N., "Alexandria Ocasio-Cortez Asks: Is It Still Ok to Have Kids in Face of Climate Change?," *Newsweek*, February 25, 2019, accessed January 30, 2020, https://www.newsweek.com/alexandria-ocasio-cortez-aoc-climate-change-have-kids-children-1342853.

69. Brown, J., "'Absolute theological bankruptcy': Union Theological Seminary students confess climate sins to plants," *Washington Examiner*, September 18, 2019, accessed September 28, 2021, https://www.washingtonexaminer.com/news/absolute-theological-bankruptcy-union-theological-seminary-students-pray-to-plants.

70. Drayer, E., "Natural wonders should have their own legal rights," *Orlando Sentinel*, December 19, 2019, accessed September 28, 2021, https://www.orlandosentinel.com/opinion/guest-commentary/os-op-nature-has-right-to-protection-20191226-l4z6jfagfbe5nctucxbzeqqnji-story.html.

71. Center, P. R., "Marriage and Cohabitation in the U.S.," *Pew Research Center*, November 6, 2019, accessed August 19, 2020, https://www.pewsocialtrends.org/2019/11/06/marriage-and-cohabitation-in-the-u-s/.

72. Kramer, S., "U.S. has world's highest rate of children living in single-parent households," *Pew Research*, December 12, 2019, accessed August 12, 2020, https://www.pewresearch.org/fact-tank/2019/12/12/u-s-children-more-likely-than-children-in-other-countries-to-live-with-just-one-parent/.

73. Graham, F., "Our Nation Has Lost Its Way," *Billy Graham Evangelistic Association*, September 27, 2012, accessed August 13, 2020, https://billygraham.org/story/our-nation-has-lost-its-way/.

74. Kumar, A., "Franklin Graham: Obama Leading America to Sinful Course; 'God Will Judge Him, Us If We Don't Repent'," *Christian Post*, June 27, 2015, accessed August 13, 2020, https://www.christianpost.com/news/franklin-graham-obama-leading-america-to-sinful-course-god-will-judge-him-us-if-we-dont-repent.html.

75. Funaro, V. "'God Will Have to Judge America' or 'Apologize to Sodom and Gomorrah' After SC Marriage Ruling, Says John Hagee," *Christian Post*, July 1, 2015, accessed August 13, 2020, https://www.christianpost.com/news/god-will-have-to-judge-america-or-apologize-to-sodom-and-gomorrah-after-sc-marriage-ruling-says-john-hagee.html.

76. Jeffress, R., "Unless There Is a Great Spiritual Revival, America's Collapse Is Inevitable," *First Baptist Church, Dallas*, October 22, 2017, accessed August 13, 2020, https://www.firstdallas.org/news/dr-robert-jeffress-unless-there-is-a-great-spiritual-revival-americas-collapse-is-inevitable/.

77. Bannister, C., "Pat Robertson: "God Will Say, 'I've Had It with America… I'm Going to Get Rid of You,'" if Equality Act Enacted," *CNS News*, May 15, 2019, accessed August 13, 2020, https://www.cnsnews.com/blog/craig-bannister/pat-robertson-god-will-say-ive-had-it-americaim-going-get-rid-you-if-equality.

78. Wilkerson, D., "The Last Days of America," *World Challenge*, June 18, 1989, accessed August 12, 2020, https://worldchallenge.org/newsletter/1989/the-last-days-of-america.

79. Wikipedia, "Wildfires in the United States," *Wikipedia*, accessed August 12, 2020, https://en.wikipedia.org/wiki/Wildfires_in_the_United_States.

80. Guinness World Records, "Highest divorce rate," *Guinness World Records*, accessed August 12, 2020, https://www.guinnessworldrecords.com/world-records/highest-divorce-rate.

81. Pew Research Center, "In U.S., Decline of Christianity Continues at Rapid Pace," *Pew Research Center*, October 17, 2019, accessed August 19, 2020, https://www.pewforum.org/2019/10/17/in-u-s-decline-of-christianity-continues-at-rapid-pace/.

82. Froelich, P., "Here are the hidden earthquake zones you don't know about," *New York Post*, December 14, 2019, accessed April 15, 2021, https://nypost.com/2019/12/14/here-are-the-hidden-earthquake-zones-you-dont-know-about/.

83. Nevett, J., "Canary Island volcano WARNING: Landslide to spark mega eruption as powerful as ATOMIC BOMB," *Daily Star*, January 22, 2018,

accessed August 19, 2020, https://www.dailystar.co.uk/news/latest-news/canary-island-volcano-cumbre-vieja-16841170.

84. Letzter, R., "A massive solar storm could wipe out almost all of our modern technology — and we'd have just hours to prepare," *Business Insider*, September 6, 2016, accessed August 19, 2020, https://finance.yahoo.com/news/157-years-ago-massive-solar-172454557.html.

85. Johnson, J., "Worldwide digital population as of January 2021," *Statista*, April 7, 2021, accessed April 20, 2021, https://www.statista.com/statistics/617136/digital-population-worldwide/.

86. Winterburn, T., "Swedes get futuristic high tech implants in their hands to replace cash and credit cars, eliminating Coronavirus contact," *Euro Weekly News*, April 10, 2020, accessed April 20, 2021, https://www.euroweeklynews.com/2020/04/10/swedes-get-futuristic-high-tech-implants-in-their-hands-to-replace-cash-and-credit-cars-eliminating-coronavirus-contact/.

87. Our World in Data, "Number of reported disaster events," *Our World in Data*, accessed April 21, 2021, https://ourworldindata.org/natural-disasters.

88. Dickerson, J. S., *Hope of Nations: Standing Strong in a Post-Truth, Post-Christian World*, Grand Rapids: Zondervan, 2018, 37.

89. Dickerson, J. S., *Hope of Nations*, 45.

90. UVA Center for Politics, "New Initiative Explores Deep, Persistent Divides Between Biden and Trump Voters," *UVA Center for Politics*, September 3, 2021, accessed November 12, 2021, https://centerforpolitics.org/crystalball/articles/new-initiative-explores-deep-persistent-divides-between-biden-and-trump-voters/.

91. Joshua Project, "Lists: All Progress Levels," *Joshua Project*, accessed April 21, 2021, https://joshuaproject.net/global/progress.

92. Wycliffe Bible Translators, "The History of Wycliffe," *Wycliffe Bible Translators*, accessed September 15, 2021, https://www.wycliffe.org/about.

93. Johsua Project, "From Every Nation," *Johsua Project*, accessed April 21, 2021, https://joshuaproject.net/assets/media/maps/from-every-nation-map.pdf.

94. Schwab, K., "Now is the time for a 'great reset'," *World Economic Forum*, June 3, 2020, accessed April 22, 2021, https://www.weforum.org/agenda/2020/06/now-is-the-time-for-a-great-reset/.

95. World Economic Forum, "8 predictions for the world in 2030," *World Economic Forum*, November 18, 2016, accessed April 22, 2021, https://www.facebook.com/watch/?v=10153920524981479.

96. Walvoord, J. F., *Every Prophecy of the Bible*, Colorado Springs, CO: David C Cook, 1999, 604.

97. Dreher, R., "Introduction: The Awakening," in *The Benedict Option: A Strategy fo Christians in a Post-Christian Nation*, New York: Sentinel, 2017, 2-3.

98. Cordero, M. "How Critical Race Theory is Dividing America," *The Heritage Foundation*, October 26 2020, accessed September 29, 2021, https://www.heritage.org/progressivism/commentary/how-critical-race-theory-dividing-america.

99. Editors of Encyclopaedia Britannica, "Totalitarianism," *Encyclopædia Britannica, Inc*, accessed April 26, 2021, https://www.britannica.com/topic/totalitarianism.

100. Peterson, A. S., "Not-so-great moments in history," *World,* February 29, 2020, https://wng.org/articles/not-so-great-moments-in-history-1617297797.

101. Murrary, D., *The Madness of Crowds: Gender, Race and Identity*, London: Bloomsbury Continuum, 2019, 119.

102. Murrary, D. in *The Madness of Crowds,* 117.

103. Flood, B. "Alex Berenson: Shutdown of Parler is Big Tech's 'most dangerous' move yet," *Fox News Channel*, January 18, 2021, accessed October 1, 2021, https://www.foxnews.com/media/parler-shutdown-dangerous-capitol-riot-berenson.

104. Bovard, R., "Court Docs Show Facebook Played Much Bigger Part In Capitol Riot Than Parler, Yet No Consequences," *The Federalist*, February 22, 2021, accessed October 1, 2021, https://thefederalist.com/2021/02/22/court-docs-show-facebook-played-much-bigger-part-in-capitol-riot-than-parler-yet-no-consequences/.

105. Prager, D., "Dennis Prager on YouTube's Record of Censorship," *Wall Street Journal*, August 6, 2021, accessed October 1, 2021, https://www.wsj.com/articles/youtube-censorship-prager-free-speech-big-tech-11628204348.

106. Wallace, A., "The Top Ten Corporate Funders of LGBTQ Issues," *Funders for LGBTQ Issues*, November 6, 2016, accessed April 28, 2021, https://lgbtfunders.org/newsposts/the-top-ten-corporate-funders-of-lgbtq-issues/.

107. Human Rights Campaign, "Corporate Equality Index 2021," *Human Rights Campaign*, accessed April 28, 2021, https://reports.hrc.org/corporate-equality-index-2021#key-findings.

108. Chase, E., "Having Sex When You're Fat: Tips on Positions, Props, and Preparation," *TeenVogue*, August 2, 2019, accessed April 28, 2021, https://www.teenvogue.com/story/fat-sex.

109. Mofokeng, T., "Why Sex Work Is Real Work," *TeenVogue*, April 26, 2019, accessed April 28, 2021, https://www.teenvogue.com/story/why-sex-work-is-real-work.

110. Liberty Counsel, "Rogue Mayor Plans Ruin, But God Brings Revival," *Liberty Counsel*, April 2, 2021, accessed September 15, 2021, https://lc.org/newsroom/details/20210402rogue-mayor-plans-ruin-but-god-brings-revival.

111. Dreher, R., *Live not by lies: A manual for Christian dissidents*, New York: Sentinel, 2020, 18.

112. Dreher, R.. *The Benedict Option: A Strategy for Christians in a Post-Christian Nation*, New York: Sentinel, 2017, 87.

113. Crockett, K., "Proof God Exists," *MakingLifeCount.net*, accessed March 4, 2021, https://s3.amazonaws.com/media.cloversites.com/fc/fcdcda31-90dd-4d9e-8256-2b8bc499f91b/documents/Proof_the_Bible_is_True.pdf.

Appendix: Fifty-Two Prophecies about Jesus[113]

He said to them, "How foolish you are, and how slow to believe all that the prophets have spoken! Did not the Messiah have to suffer these things and then enter his glory?" And beginning with Moses and all the Prophets, he explained to them what was said in all the Scriptures. (Luke 24:25–27)

Prophecies in the Old Testament about the Messiah	Old Testament Prophecy Verses	Approximate Date Prophesied	New Testament Fulfillment Verses
He would be born of a virgin	Isaiah 7:14	740–680 BC	Matthew1:18–25
He would be the Son of God	Psalm 2:7	1000 BC	Matthew 3:17
He would be a descendant of Abraham	Genesis 12:3, 22:18	1400 BC	Matthew 1:1
The Messiah would be a descendant of Isaac	Genesis 21:12	1400 BC	Matthew 1:2; Luke 3:34
The Messiah would be a descendant of Jacob	Numbers 24:17	1400 BC	Matthew 1:2; Luke 3:34
He would be from tribe of Judah	Genesis 49:10	1400 BC	Matthew 1:2; Luke 3:33
He would be from the family of Jesse	Isaiah 11:1	740–680 BC	Matthew 1:6; Luke 3:32
The Messiah would be from house of David	Jeremiah 23:5	627–580 BC	Matthew 1:1; Luke 3:31
He would be raised up as a prophet like Moses	Deuteronomy 18:15, 18	1400 BC	Acts 3:22; 7:37
The Messiah would be born in Bethlehem	Micah 5:2	722 BC	Matthew 2:1

Prophecies in the Old Testament about the Messiah	Old Testament Prophecy Verses	Approximate Date Prophesied	New Testament Fulfillment Verses
After He was born, babies would be killed in Bethlehem	Jeremiah 31:15	627–580 BC	Matthew 2:16–18
He would be called Immanuel, meaning "God with us"	Isaiah 7:14	740–680 BC	Matthew 1:23
He would be called out of Egypt (Joseph and Mary fled to Egypt with Jesus)	Hosea 11:1	720 BC	Matthew 2:15
The Messiah would come from Galilee	Isaiah 9:1–2	740–680 BC	Matthew 4:13–16
The Spirit of the Lord would be upon Him	Isaiah 61:1	740–680 BC	Luke 4:16–21; Matthew 12:17–18
He would be preceded by a messenger	Malachi 3:1	430 BC	Matthew 11:10
He would do miracles	Isaiah 35:5–6	740–680 BC	Matthew 11:2–5
Israel's king would ride into Jerusalem on donkey	Zechariah 9:9	470 BC	Matthew 21:5–9; John 12:14–15
The Messiah would be welcomed with "Blessed is He who comes in the name of the Lord"	Psalm 118:26	1000 BC	John 12:13
He would be hated for no reason	Psalm 35:19; 69:4	1000 BC	John 15:25
He would be rejected by the religious rulers	Psalm 118:22	1000 BC	Matthew 21:42
He would be rejected by His own brothers	Psalm 69:8	1000 BC	John 7:5
He would be betrayed by a friend	Psalm 41:9	1000 BC	Matthew 10:4
His betrayer would eat bread with Him	Psalm 41:9	1000 BC	John 13:18, 26
He would be betrayed for money—30 pieces of silver. Predicted exactly 30 pieces (not 29 or 31). The coins would be silver, not gold.	Zechariah 11:12	470 BC	Matthew 26:15
The money would be returned	Zechariah 11:12–13	470 BC	Matthew 27:3
The money would be thrown in the house of the Lord	Zechariah 11:13	470 BC	Matthew 27:5
The betrayal money would pay for a Potter's field	Zechariah 11:13	470 BC	Matthew 27:7
He would be forsaken by the disciples	Zechariah 13:7	470 BC	Matthew 26:31, 56
He would be silent before His accusers	Isaiah 53:7	740–680 BC	Matthew 26:62–63

Prophecies in the Old Testament about the Messiah	Old Testament Prophecy Verses	Approximate Date Prophesied	New Testament Fulfillment Verses
The Messiah would be mocked	Isaiah 53:3	740–680 BC	Matthew 27:29
He would be beaten with a rod	Micah 5:1	722 BC	Mark 15:19
He would be spat upon in the face	Isaiah 50:6	740–680 BC	Mark 14:65
The Messiah would be wounded, bruised	Isaiah 53:5	740–680 BC	Matt. 27:30; Luke 22:63
The Messiah would be scourged on His back	Isaiah 50:6, 53:5	740–680 BC	John 19:1
His hands and feet would be pierced	Psalm 22:16	1000 BC	John 20:25
His garments would be divided	Psalm 22:18	1000 BC	John 19:23
They would cast lots for His clothing	Psalm 22:18	1000 BC	John 19:24
The Messiah would die with criminals	Isaiah 53:12	740–680 BC	Mark 15:28; Luke 22:37
Those watching the crucifixion would wag their heads	Psalm 22:7; 109:25	1000 BC	Mark 15:29; Matthew 27:39
Those watching the crucifixion would mock Him for not saving Himself	Psalm 22:8	1000 BC	Matthew 27:41–43
He would pray for those crucifying Him	Isaiah 53:12	740–680 BC	Luke 23:34
He would be given vinegar to drink	Psalm 69:21	1000 BC	Matthew 27:34
"Why hast thou forsaken me?"	Psalm 22:1	1000 BC	Matthew 27:46
"Into thine hand I commit my spirit"	Psalm 31:5	1000 BC	Luke 23:46
His side would be pierced	Zechariah 12:10	470 BC	John 19:34, 37
None of the Messiah's bones would be broken	Psalm 34:20	1000 BC	John 19:32–36
He would be buried in a rich man's tomb	Isaiah 53:9	740–680 BC	Matthew 27:57–60
He would be dead for three days and three nights	Jonah 1:17	760 BC	Matthew 12:40
He would descend into hell	Psalm 16:10; 49:15	1000 BC	Acts 2:27, 31; Ephesians 4:9
The Messiah would be resurrected from dead	Psalm 16:10; 30:3	1000 BC	Acts 2:31; 13:33–35
Through His resurrection He would swallow up death in victory	Isaiah 25:8	740–680 BC	1 Corinthians 15:54
He would ascend into heaven	Psalm 68:18	1000 BC	Acts 1:9; Ephesians 4:8–10

Prophecies in the Old Testament about the Messiah	Old Testament Prophecy Verses	Approximate Date Prophesied	New Testament Fulfillment Verses
He would be seated at the right hand of the Father in heaven	Psalm 110:1	1000 BC	Acts 2:34–35; Colossians 3:1
He would be a priest according to the order of Melchizedek	Psalm 110:4	1000 BC	Hebrews 5:6, 10; 6:20
The Messiah would be a light to the entire world, including non-Jews	Isaiah 42:6; 49:6	740–680 BC	Luke 2:32; Acts 13:47

Index

About the Authors

David L. Johnson is a former college teacher with a PhD in education. He has served for many years in a prison ministry, is a certified chaplain, and is a member of a large nondenominational evangelical church in the Twin Cities, Minnesota.

Richard A. Hansen is a retired commercial airline pilot. He has served for many years in a prison ministry and a nursing home ministry, is a licensed chaplain, and is also a member of the same church in the Twin Cities.

Contact Us
By mail:
Training Guide Ministry
P.O. Box 533
Shakopee, MN 55379
Online:
TrainingGuideMinistry.com
Info@TrainingGuideMinistry.com

Other Books by the Authors

Training Guide for Heaven: Running for the Prize
This 126-page book urges readers to spend more time planning for their life after death then they do planning for a vacation. The authors show how to visualize your goals in the afterlife, earn rewards in heaven, keep your eyes on the prize, and make the best use of your time on earth.

Study Guide
This 129-page companion study guide for *Training Guide for Heaven: Running for the Prize* provides a lesson for each chapter of the book. Each lesson provides key points at a glance, application discussion questions for each key point, a going deeper question, and a quiz with answers.

Printed in the United States
by Baker & Taylor Publisher Services